Youth Specialties
www.YouthSpecialties.com

ZONDERVAN
WWW.ZONDERVAN.COM

exploring spirituality and contemplative practices in youth ministry

soul shaper

tony jones

Soul Shaper: Exploring Spirituality and Comtemplative Practices in Youth Ministry

Copyright © 2003 by Youth Specialties

Youth Specialties Books, 300 South Pierce Street, El Cajon, California 92020, are published by Zondervan Publishing House, 5300 Patterson Avenue Southeast, Grand Rapids, Michigan 49530.

Library of Congress Cataloging-in-Publication Data

Jones, Tony, 1968-
    Soul shaper : exploring spirituality and contemplative practices
  in youth ministry / by Tony Jones.
        p. cm.
    Includes bibliographical references.
    ISBN 0-310-25101-X (pbk.)
    1. Church work with youth.   2. Spiritual life--Christianity.
I.
  Title.
  BV4447.J665 2003
  259'.23--dc21

2002155550

Web site addresses listed in this book were current at the time of publication. Please contact Youth Specialties via e-mail (YS@YouthSpecialties.com) to report URLs that are no longer operational and replacement URLs if available.

Edited by Lois Swagerty

Cover and interior design by Proxy

Printed in the United States of America

04 05 06 07 / / 10 9 8 7 6 5 4 3

DEDICATED TO LILY

Daughter of my heart

WARNING: ~~DO NOT~~ TRY THIS AT HOME

This is a strange book. It is a book about spiritual exercises and their application in the practice of youth ministry, but I don't want you to apply them. At least, not yet. To take a chapter from this book and think, "Hey, I wonder how I can implement Centering Prayer this Wednesday night with my junior highers…" would do a great injustice to the saints of the Christian church who have over the past two millennia labored at practicing and perfecting these disciplines.

So before you implement them, *please* practice them. *These are not gimmicks.* This is not an Ideas book or a discussion starter book or a great-games-for-over-50-kids-in-a-gym book. Those books are all great and necessary—we all have those weeks when we need a last-minute idea for youth group. But this is not one of those books.

In fact, I am quite sure that this book is an injustice to those saints I mention. This book is not thorough; it is a primer. And, as such, it is a cursory glance at more than a dozen different spiritual practices that have their roots deep in the history of the church. You will not come close to learning everything you need to know about any of the practices delineated below, but hopefully you'll get enough of an idea to see which ones you would like to pursue further. In that case, I hope the resources section in the back helps you develop these practices.

The fact is, you may be a couple of years from utilizing any of these practices in your youth ministry. *It is absolutely mandatory that a practice first become a part of your life before you try it with your students.* Take this advice to heart: These exercises are not to be trifled with or plugged in to a 15-minute slot at the fall retreat.

If, however, you find one or two that you incorporate into your rule of life, I am quite sure that you and the students God has put into your care will be eternally changed as a result.

For that reason, this book is written to you, the youth worker, and it details how you can incorporate these disciplines in *your* life. God bless you.

TJ

Contents

Preface   08

Part I: Introduction

01 New Paradigms in Youth Ministry   12
02 What Is **Spirituality** and How   24
    Do You **Practice** It?

Part II: Via Contemplativa
Contemplative Approaches to Spirituality

03 Sacred Reading   36
04 Silence and Solitude   48
05 The Jesus Prayer   60
06 Centering Prayer   72
07 Meditation   84
08 The Ignatian Examen   98
09 Icons   108
10 Spiritual Direction   120
11 The Daily Office   132

Part III: Via Activa
Bodily Approaches to Spirituality

12	The Labyrinth	144
13	Stations of the Cross	154
14	Pilgrimage	170
15	Fasting	184
16	The Sign of the Cross and Other Bodily Prayers	198
17	Sabbath	208
18	Service	222

Epilogue: Developing a Rule of Life	232
Book Resources	236
Web Resources	243
Bibliography	247
Some Devotional Classics in the Christian Tradition	251

PREFACE

It seems to me that most authors wait until the end of their preface to say that "without my spouse this book wouldn't have been possible." I'll say it right now: my wife, Julie, is my biggest fan, and, if this were a just world, she would have coauthor credits on this book. When I write, it doubles her workload at home, and yet she steadfastly encourages me and exhorts me onward. Our children, Tanner and Lily, have also been a blessing in the past months. Although Lily is too little to understand where Daddy's going with a laptop and a box of books, two-year-old Tanner knows that "Daddy going to coffee shop to write story." I cannot thank the three of them enough.

The majority of the research and writing for the book you are about to read took place whilst I was on a three-month sabbatical from my pastoral duties at Colonial Church. Having reached my five-year anniversary on staff, the congregation and my co-workers were gracious enough to grant me that time set apart for rest and writing. The bulk of the extra work landed on the shoulders of my fellow youth workers, Tim Inman, Julie Ramsland, and Sherry Chapman—thank you!

Further, I was given a generous grant by the Louisville Institute, and I thank them and the Lilly Endowment which funds them.

The Louisville grant allowed me to travel to Europe, take Julie on a five-year-anniversary trip, visit Fuller and Princeton Seminaries, go on Youth Specialties' Sabbath Retreat, and buy dozens and dozens of books.

Numerous individuals were both hospitable and helpful to me on my travels. In England, I was taken in by good souls like Jonny Baker, Pete Ward, Andy Freeman, and Dave Tomlinson, and in Dublin I was overwhelmed by the gracious reception I received from Fr. Alan McGuckian and the rest of the staff at the Jesuit Communication Centre. Shane and Andrea Hipps and Jen and Jess Elmquist gave me places to sleep in California, and Kenda Dean warmly welcomed me at Princeton. My co-pilgrims at the Sabbath Retreat in May 2002 and at the Villa Maria Center in Frontenac, Minnesota deeply influenced me with things said and unsaid. Conversations with Nancey Murphy, Mark Lau Branson, Craig Detweiler, and Miroslav Volf left impressions as well.

The Youth Specialties staff is unparalleled. Their commitment to me and to youth ministry makes writing a joy. I thank Mark Oestreicher for his leadership and encouragement, Dave Urbanski for his admirable project direction, Will Penner for his guidance of *Youthworker*, Beth Slevcove for her pioneering work in spiritual direction for youth workers, to Tic Long and Michelle Fockler for allowing me to work out my thoughts at the conventions, and Mike and Karla Yaconelli for their spiritual leadership of the entire organization. (And, as an editor, Lois Swagerty is a joy to work with!)

Youth Specialties' Web guru, Mike Atkinson, sent out a request from me to over 40,000 youth workers in his weekly e-mail. As a result, I have been blessed to correspond with dozens of youth workers who graciously and without expecting any reward offered me ideas, wisdom, and cautions. God knows of your selfless ministry, and God will use your ideas to continue building his kingdom. Please know that there are many others like you who are working tirelessly to bring the Good News of Jesus Christ to students in innovative and ancient ways.

My "fellows" at Emergent continue to be a great source of strength and koinonia—they are some of the sharpest people around, trying to drag the church, kicking and screaming, into the postmodern era: Brian McLaren, Doug Pagitt, Chris Seay, Tim Keel, Tim Conder, Brad Cecil, Ivy Beckwith, Rudy Carrasco, and Laci Scott.

My thanks to individuals who lent their expertise and proofread chapters, pointing out my glaring errors: Phyllis Tickle, Frederica Matthewes-Green, Alan McGuckian, Jill Hartwell Geffrion, Fr. Nicholas Speier, Jay Folley, and Pat McKee.

Finally, the middle school, high school, and college students of Colonial Church are an exceptional group—in these last six years they have been both friends and guinea pigs as our youth staff has attempted to forge a new paradigm for youth ministry. For all of the ideas that missed, sorry; for the ones that worked, you students deserve much of the credit. Although it's unfair to single anyone out, I want to especially thank Charlie McGlynn and Katy Lund, both of whom have come to every weird incense-and-Gregonian-chant prayer service we've had.

I humbly offer what follows as a co-laborer in the gospel. These last months have been a tremendous journey in my life, and I know that I will never be the same. I pray that this little book will be received as a small contribution to the ever-expanding Kingdom of God.

Pax et Bonum,
Tony Jones
Feast of St. James the Greater
July 25, 2002

Chapter 01
New Paradigms in Youth Ministry

Old habits are hard to break, and no one is easily weaned from his own opinions; but if you rely on your own reasoning and ability rather than on the virtue of submission to Jesus Christ, you will but seldom and slowly attain wisdom. For God wills that we become perfectly obedient to himself, and that we transcend mere reason on the wings of burning love for him.

Thomas à Kempis

I wrote a lot of this book in coffee shops. I was working at one in May when one of those Midwestern spring thunderstorms came roiling across the plains of western Minnesota. The table at which I was sitting overlooked a large parking lot for an adjacent mall. As the wind picked up, the trees started to bend, and then the rain came in almost horizontal sheets.

The mall's parking lot was only half full, being a weekday afternoon. Way out on the edge was parked a brand new BMW 525i —it didn't even have license plates yet. Someone had parked it far away from all other cars, hoping to avoid the dings and dents of carelessly opened doors.

As the wind gusted, I saw a shopping cart begin to roll, pushed by the storm. Free from the constraints of the Cart Corral, the unmanned missile gained speed, unhindered by obstacles as it wheeled across the slick asphalt.

I saw it coming—it seemed to be caught in the tractor beam of the new car—250 yards and closing fast! 200 yards! 150! 100 yards! 50...25...10...5...Impact! That cart smashed right into the side of the as-yet unblemished BMW. I kid you not: there was not another car within 100 yards, but that cart was homed right to its target. Mission accomplished.

It seems to me that God is a lot like that shopping cart—not that God has four wheels and a child safety strap, but that God always seeks us out. No matter how far away we park, and no matter how much we try to avoid conflict with him, God finds us and leaves his mark. It's not a search-and-destroy mission; it's a search-and-give-life mission.

That's not to say that we can't avoid God. Of course we can, and a lot of people do. But for those of us who are followers of Christ, and especially for those of us called to lead others into Christ's presence, it's pretty common for God to hunt us down and smack us in the right front quarter panel. Hence the continued popularity of Frances Thompson's poem, "The Hounds of Heaven," in which the protagonist proclaims,

I fled Him, down the nights and down the days;
I fled Him, down the arches of the years;
I fled Him, down the labyrinthine ways
Of my own mind; and in the mist of tears
I hid from Him, and under running laughter.

And yet Love pursues with an "unhurried pace," and a Voice proclaims, "Naught shelters thee, who wilt not shelter Me." Love wins; God wins, hounding us toward the gates of heaven,

WHERE WE'VE COME FROM

never giving up on us, in spite of our attempts to outrun him.

God has been pursuing each of us, and I believe he has been pursuing the profession of youth ministry.

Youth ministry has undergone a significant amount of change in the last 30 years. The fact that I can refer to what we do as a "profession" is foremost among the changes. We've come a long way from the days when Mike Yaconelli and Wayne Rice were selling mimeographed game sheets out of the backs of their cars. The number of "youth ministry packs" of those marketing postcards you get in the mail bespeaks the influence that we have in the Christian marketplace.

Youth ministry has morphed from a fringe occupation to a "must-have" for any church that wants to influence its community. In the heady days of the 1980s and 1990s, the number of job openings in churches suddenly and vastly outnumbered the number of qualified individuals to take those jobs—and that trend continues today.

But somewhere in those years, youth ministry lost its way. It became about personalities rather than about relationships. Churches looking for a new youth pastor were unabashed in their desire to have someone with a "strong personality." Not unlike the Pony Express, the best candidates for youth ministry jobs were young, single men—men who would literally sacrifice their own social lives to work 70 hours a week for $18,000 a year. And if you happened to work for a parachurch organization, you had to raise that salary yourself.

This engendered an atmosphere of self-assured entrepreneurs, almost reckless in their desire to grow a big ministry. And the fact is, you often grow a big ministry by having a big personality. Workshops popped up in the 1980s and 1990s teaching youth pastors how to be "dynamic communicators," and the question you heard around the conventions was, "What are you running?"—meaning, "How big is your youth group?"

Pardon the cliché, but size mattered. Job announcements even publicized the fact that a church was looking for a youth worker who could "manage a large ministry with hundreds of kids and dozens of volunteers." Youth workers were reading more books on management and leadership than on youth culture. Some youth pastors even became consumed with architecture as they planned how to build the new youth wing on the church.

I am deliberately painting with a broad brush, and you may resent the paint I've splattered on you. However, we cannot deny that these trends were common in student ministry at the end of the 20th century. In fact, it's been these very emphases that Mike Yaconelli has targeted in his "Dangerous Wonder" column in the back of *Youthworker* for several years.

But the days of big programming, dynamic communicators, and huge sound systems is coming to an end. As youth ministry comes of age, and more youth workers are graying in the job (as opposed to jumping to a "real" ministry), the allure of spotlights and microphones is waning. Many Christian colleges and seminaries are taking youth ministry seriously enough to provide professors who reflect theologically on youth work, so more theologically astute individuals are entering the field. And if one thing has been proven time and time again, it's that a long-term relationship, not big programming, nurtures a student's faith in Christ.

WHERE WE ARE

Currently, youth ministry is undergoing a revolution. Or better yet, a renaissance. And it is this new era that God's "hounds of heaven" have been hounding us into. It is a renaissance of creativity and innovation—and like any renaissance, it is drawing on the best of the past.

Youth pastors and the institutions that provide for us are changing. People are harking back to the spiritual disciplines and to the classic, orthodox theology that have defined the church for centuries, and they are applying what they find to the practice of youth ministry.

Honestly, the best way for me to validate the reality and essence of this change is to provide a bunch of examples, first on the institutional level:

→ The Lilly Endowment, a private, family foundation in Indianapolis, has given millions of dollars to seminaries, colleges, and other organizations for the development of programs that introduce students to classic theology and to classic spiritual disciplines.

→ The Youth Ministry and Spirituality Project at San Francisco Theological Seminary is in the midst of a multiyear program to teach classic disciplines to youth pastors, volunteer leaders, and students. Currently, they are working with 13 churches and 10 denominational leaders, and they periodically report what they have learned at consultations and in print.

→ Upper Room Books has published *Way to Live: Christian Practices for Teens*, a book detailing 18 practices such as what to do with your stuff, telling the truth, being welcoming, and grieving. Eighteen students and 18 adults collaborated on this project over two years. Due in 2003 is *Sharing a Way to Live with Teens*, a sequel for youth workers detailing the undergirding theology of the practices and giving ideas for their application.

→ Youth Specialties offers a Labyrinth experience at each of their National Youth Workers Conventions. They have also hired a full-time spiritual director, and they offer free spiritual direction at the conventions. They offer numerous Sabbath retreats every year for youth workers to take some time for silence and learn some spiritual disciplines. And this book is part of their SoulShaper line, of which YS President Mark Oestreicher writes, "By using historic contemplative practices and fleshing them out in the context of modern youth ministry, we're not just connecting kids to God in real and tangible ways—we're also connecting kids to God's unfolding story."

→ The Anglican Church in England has hired Jonny Baker, inventor of the Labyrinth Experience detailed in Chapter 12, to find new ways to engage British students in Christian spirituality.

And much is happening as well at the local church and parachurch level. My thanks to the many youth workers who sent me their ideas and innovations for inclusion. Here are some that were e-mailed to me and some that I visited:

→ The Boiler Room in Reading, England is housed in a former pub on the spot of a medieval monastery—in fact, they call themselves a "Millennium Three Monastery." Not your average drop-in center for teens, the Boiler Room has people committed to pray 24 hours a day, seven days a week (part of a larger 24-7 prayer movement in the UK). They have a pilgrimage flat (in which I stayed on my visit), rooms for local youth groups to meet, and multiple prayer chapels. Their online "wailing wall" is a place where students from all over the world can post prayer requests, and the pray-ers at the Boiler Room bring those requests before God.

→ Chad Farrand is a youth pastor in Michigan. His senior high students learned the *lectio divina* method of praying with Scripture in seventh grade, and in a recent congregational poll, these students had the highest rate of daily devotions in the church—higher even than the church elders. Chad e-mailed me this: "Just last week, we were going out to bowl, and one of my freshmen asked, 'Now, we are going to be doing *lectio divina* and some solitude next week, right?' Man, that means so much! These kids crave closeness with God!"

→ Lilly Lewin in Ohio produced a Prayer Room SOS for a weekend retreat. Over the course of 12 stations, students were guided through prayer for themselves, others, and the world, all centered around Isaiah 61. Sweet and sour candies reminded students of the good and bad in life as they prayed for their hometown of Cincinnati; neon-colored sticky notes on windows made a type of stained glass of prayer requests; pieces of broken dishes stuccoed mosaic-style on a wall reminded students of their brokenness. Lilly's goal: "To create an experiential prayer and worship center for use by the students and staff of SOS utilizing tangible mediums to engage all five senses in prayer and worship;" and her purpose: "To encourage prayer in new and exciting ways and to teach us to engage in prayer for personal, local, and global needs."

→ Jeremy Vickers in Pennsylvania wrote, "I ask my youth to fast or give something up/take something on during Lent, and I was shocked to hear that some other youth ministers and churches don't even talk about Lent. I know many Christians now do not like to follow the Christian year, but I believe that it is vital to the life of our youth. Ancient practices in the church seem to be gaining in popularity, especially in the last five years. I know this is not innovative, but it works. Our youth come out of Lent with a greater appreciation of what they have and who they are. This also helps on mission trips when their intake of food changes for a week or so. Along the same lines, our Survivor trip last year had a similar goal. We left for three days, camped out, no batteries, no watches, nothing technological, and they had challenges, cooked for themselves, read their Bibles and learned what it means to live in a world of beauty and nature. Quite an interesting trip. Kind of an extreme camp out. It changed a few lives."

→ Brad Miller works in California: "One of the most incredible things we have done in our Sunday evening services is to try to create an environment conducive to experiencing God. After studying God's Word, we turn down the lights and leave the candles on the tables as the only lights in the room. We begin to worship. We have 2 separate areas in the back of the church that are sort of 'God-business stations.' At each station there is a 6-foot tall cross, communion elements, a tray of tea lights (that can be symbolically lit when lifting up our prayers to God), and a few large candles that provide just enough light. We are very deliberate about inviting everyone to worship God in their own way. We let them know that at any time during worship they can go back to the cross and do their business with God. What is amazing is to see how passionately and sincerely people are connecting with God at those stations. When we give them the freedom to just 'be,' they do. It is a beautiful sight to behold."

→ Jonathan Gonyou assigns his senior highers a chapter a week from Richard Foster's *Celebration of Discipline*. He finds the students almost always rise to the challenge of practicing each particular discipline.

→ Richard Logan in Texas brings his students on a weekend SOLO retreat, during which they observe lengthy periods of silence, solitude, and fasting.

→ Eric Haskins in Illinois has three levels at the annual "Weekend of the Disciplines." Students experience silence and solitude, communion, fasting, and more. His whole ministry has taken the disciplines on as the guiding model.

I could go on and on, simply quoting e-mails I have received and people with whom I have spoken. But I hope these examples are enough to convince you of the renaissance taking place in youth ministry.

WHERE WE'RE GOING

I'm no futurist. And most of the futurists I've heard are full of something. But there's a lot to be hopeful about in the turn that youth ministry has taken. And I hope this book, at least, will be another piece of evidence that we're moving in the right direction. Nothing on the horizon seems to indicate we'll move back to the personality-driven entertainment model of the late 20th century; most evidence indicates we are moving into a new and hopeful place.

Not all is rosy, however. In the midst of my correspondence in preparing this book, there are a couple of strongly worded cautionary e-mails. One warned that introducing spiritual disciplines to youth, when done wrong, can be very damaging. A Young Life credo is, "It's a sin to bore a kid with the gospel"— the same thing can be said of spiritual practices. To teach students about an ancient discipline in a way that isn't relevant to their lives and their faith will turn them away from that discipline and maybe all disciplines. We dare not make that mistake.

Another caution came from a person who is afraid that youth workers will jump on the "Spiritual Paradigm" bandwagon because it's the next big thing. Just like "seeker sensitive" or "youth-led worship" or "cell groups" or "postmodern worship,"

ABOUT THIS BOOK

this new movement could be abducted by publishing houses and youth ministry "experts" and "consultants." His well-founded fear is that youth workers won't take the time to develop these disciplines in their own lives, but will simply plug them in at opportune times during the programming year. He may be right, but I hope he's not.

Where we go from here will be up to us who are committed to this profession. And the more of us who stay for an extended period of time in this line of work, preferably at the same church, the better. We will be able to develop relationships with students and families over time. They will get to see our lives and we will get inside their lives. If we can stay put for a while, our students and their families will see us living our lives with integrity, working on our relationships and marriages, doing our best to raise children who love the Lord, being wise stewards of our money, etc.

Eugene Peterson has said, "I think the most important thing a pastor does is who he or she is." [Bailey 4] My pastor said a similar thing to me at my annual review a couple years ago: "As a pastor on this staff, I care a lot more about who you are than about what you do." Ultimately, it's all about how we live, you and me, in the midst of this ministry.

For that very reason, this book is long on history and theology and short on ways you might apply these practices in your ministry this week. I want *you* to be changed by prayer, fasting, solitude, etc. Then, if you wish, you can introduce them to your students in myriad ways. If I were to give lots of examples, it would perpetuate two fallacies: 1) that I'm some kind of expert at introducing these practices to students, and 2) that these are the best (or only) ways to use them. This paradigm, if it is that, is still being written and invented by all of us.

Remember those programmers I listed a few pages ago? *They* are the innovators—you would do well to list yourself among *them*. I'm not nearly that innovative—honestly, most of the great ideas in our ministry come from other people on the staff. And the bottom line is, *you* know your students. Not me. Not any other author. You! Knowing your students as you do, you can decide the best ways to introduce spiritual disciplines to them.

What I can try to do, however, is shed some light on the history of the church. Whereas most of the ideas you read about above are new, all of the practices you will read about below are old—most are very old. Many of them have been lost to the whole church, or at least to part of the church over time. It's time for us to recover what has been so important to the spiritual development of hundreds of saints over dozens of centuries.

One of the things you may have to leave at the front cover is denominational bigotry. A lot of the practices herein will seem very "Catholic" or very "Eastern Orthodox," and if you aren't from one of those traditions, remember this: before 1054 we were all Catholic/Orthodox! That's right—for the first half of Christian history, there was one church, and most of the practices in this book are from that time. You've probably met someone who, when asked "What denomination are you?" responded, "I'm Christian." Well, when these practices were being developed, everyone could say that.

The following chapter is further introduction, including thoughts on spirituality and the practice thereof. Then comes the meat of the book: 16 ancient practices. The practices are divided into two sections. Those in *Via Contemplativa* are practices that rely on bodily quiet and stillness. For most of them you sit, and for all of them you primarily engage the spirit. *Via Activa* describes practices in which you engage the body, whether it be by depriving it of food (e.g., fasting) or walking (e.g., Stations of the Cross).

While this division of body and spirit, and the corresponding disciplines, is ancient, it's also a false dichotomy. Because, of course, to practice the stillness required for Centering Prayer takes an enormous amount of physical discipline—one must use the mind (a physical object) to bring the body to rest and to tune out all possible distractions. And to walk a labyrinth, while it is physical, is also deeply spiritual. However artificial, though, the division stands, for it may be somewhat helpful.

Each chapter begins with a quote from Thomas à Kempis' *The Imitation of Christ*, quite possibly the greatest—and surely the most widely read—Christian spiritual classic after the Bible.

Each chapter also has several sections. The first is an opening anecdote, either from my own life and ministry or, more often, from someone else's. I hope these stories will help bring these practices to life and pull you into their snare.

Next is a section on the history of the practice, not only because I love history, but because we do a great disservice to a discipline and the faithful Christians who have practiced it when we do not consider from whence it came. Indeed, I find that students are far more interested in trying a practice when they know the story behind it.

Theology is the next part of each chapter. In order for us to practice these spiritual disciplines with integrity, we must decide for ourselves if they are theologically defensible within our own traditions. The use of icons for prayer, for instance, has a long and contentious theological history. And the labyrinth, because of its pre-Christian origins and its use by the New Age movement, is avoided in some traditions. Obviously, I have included no practices with which I'm theologically uncomfortable, but you will have to make those determinations for yourself.

Next is a section on practice, giving some general guidelines for the application of the discipline; these have been honed over the centuries by thousands of Christians. Then there are some cursory thoughts on how a practice might be applied in youth ministry. For reasons stated above, this section is usually quite short—in fact, it should be completely blank, for you to fill in.

In most of the chapters I also include journal snippets from my direct experiences—over several months and several countries—learning more about these spiritual exercises. I hope my personal takes on these disciplines will help clothe them in flesh, blood, and soul for you.

Finally, since I don't deserve to have the last word on any of these disciplines, there is a word from someone much wiser than I to conclude each chapter.

In closing, at the risk of repeating myself, this is a book for you. My hope is that you'll be transformed by one or two of these practices, as I have been, and that consequently you'll be a better youth pastor. Try them, experiment, dive in, and see where God takes you.

Chapter 02

What Is Spirituality and How Do You Practice It?

If you wish to live in peace and harmony with others, you must learn to discipline yourself in many ways.

Thomas à Kempis

Let's be honest—the term *spirituality* has gotten a bad reputation in some Christian camps. Maybe it's the fact that since the Enlightenment, intellectual knowledge, theology, and doctrine have been primary. Maybe it's because the term was co-opted by the New Age movement in the late 20th century. No matter why, some Christians, evangelicals foremost among them, have shied away from this word.

However, it's time to take *spirituality* back, and put the word *Christian* in front of it. Christian spirituality has a long and illustrious history, out of which grew all of the practices outlined in this book. Any number of definitions of spirituality abound, so we'll consider just three.

→ A fairly academic definition comes from Alister McGrath: "Christian spirituality concerns the quest for a fulfilled and authentic Christian existence, involving the bringing together of the fundamental ideas of Christianity and the whole experience of living on the basis of and within the scope of the Christian faith." [McGrath 2]

→ Presbyterian pastor Marjorie Thompson prefers the more biblical phrase, "the spiritual life," which she describes as "simply the increasing vitality and sway of God's Spirit in us." [Thompson 6]

→ Seventeenth-century mystic Brother Lawrence had a definition that's simpler yet: "the practice of the presence of God."

Spirituality is derived from 'spirit' (*ruach* in the Old Testament; *pneuma* in the New Testament), so it clearly has connections with God's Holy Spirit, the third person of the Trinity. The Spirit hovered over the face of the waters at the genesis of the world, gave Jesus his power to heal, gave birth to the church at Pentecost, and dwells with believers as the "Advocate" that Jesus promised. *To be enlivened by God's Spirit, then, is the goal of Christian spirituality.*

No matter what one's theological disposition, it's clear that the protagonist in this relationship is God. God's Spirit, as Jesus told Nicodemus, is like the wind—though we know it's there, we don't know where it came from or where it's going. The Spirit moves at God's whim, and, as the Lord reminded Job, God's ways are often not comprehensible by mortals. The history of revivals (in all Christian traditions) points to one fact: when and where the Holy Spirit moves is neither predictable nor controllable.

A RELATIONSHIP

However, we human beings do have a role; a unique aspect of Christianity is that because of Jesus Christ and the Holy Spirit, we have a relationship with the Creator of the cosmos. Marjorie Thompson's definition of "the spiritual life" goes on, "It is a magnificent choreography of the Holy Spirit in the human spirit, moving us toward communion with both Creator and creation. The spiritual life is thus grounded in relationship. It has to do with God's way of relating to us and our way of responding to God." [Thompson 6]

Human beings play an active role in spirituality, for we seek to come inside or under God's Spirit—or to have God's Spirit come inside us to dwell. All of the interest in spirituality and religion (organized or unorganized) is a result of what Blaise Pascal called the "infinite abyss" within each of us, which "can only be filled by an infinite and immutable object, that is to say, only by God himself." [Pascal 154] While we may scoff at some of the upstart religions, cults, sects, and gurus, they are popular and successful because people are *seeking*. People want, as Thompson writes, communion with the Creator.

In this way, Christians are no different than any other group or individual—we're on a quest, we're seekers. Those Christians who walk around smug in their certainty that they've got it all figured out, that the quest is over, might well hear Jesus' words to Peter ringing in their ears: "Get behind me, Satan!" [Matthew 16:23; Mark 8:33] Of course, Christians have a unique relationship with God via Jesus Christ, but our mission to be ever more indwelt by the Holy Spirit is ongoing.

This search has driven countless men and women into the desert—we know them as the Desert Fathers and Mothers. It has driven others into monasteries and convents. Others have gone to the mission field or into caves or into communes to pursue a deeper communion with God. Some have sought it in community, others in seclusion.

Our age is no different. People are still seeking. The middle school and high school students with whom we work are foremost among those seekers. The Internet generation is seeking—searches for God and spiritual matters are some of the most popular on the Web. And students are inundated with spiritual choices—the humanities class at our local high school spends almost one-third of the semester hearing guest speakers from just about every religious persuasion you've ever heard of.

TEENAGE SPIRITUALITY

Patricia Hersch, in her masterful work on high school culture, *A Tribe Apart*, begins with the story of a boy from Reston, Virginia who, the week before he started his senior year, went on a Native American-style "vision quest." Jonathan spent four days on the top of a bluff with only a blanket, a loaf of bread, and a native drum. He was up there to receive his vision, his life's calling. He was, for all intents and purposes, up there to have communion with the Creator.

As Jonathan recounted his time on the mountaintop, Hersch was struck with how his vision quest was a perfect metaphor for American adolescence:

Adolescence is a journey, a search for self in every dimension of being. It is about dreams, fears, and hopes, as much as about hormones, SAT scores, and fashion. It is about endless possibilities as well as dead ends. It is searching, testing, experimentation. It is growth: it is undeniable that the young person at any one point in time will be different one year later—different physically, intellectually, emotionally, and experientially. [Hersch 17]

And we might easily add "and spiritually" to that list. Kids are constantly searching, exploring, and questioning about spiritual matters. Their spiritual identity isn't set—it's Silly Putty, not concrete. And especially at the time we get them, in middle school and high school, most of them are spurning *anything* that comes from their parents. They consider themselves explorers, spiritual Lewises and Clarks, off to discover new lands and map them out (and if their spiritual explorations drive their parents a little crazy, all the better).

Much has been written about the common response these days, "I'm not religious, I'm spiritual." And you only have to ask about three high school students in a random sampling before you get that or a similar phrase. There's also an undeniable interest among young people in ancient and medieval times. Medieval role-playing games continue to be popular, as do the *Lord of the Rings* books and movies. The Goth movement of a few years ago was a postmodern blend of Middle Ages apparel, occult themes, and heavy rock music. Within Christianity, "postmodern worship" is often characterized by medieval polyphonic chants, incense, and wrought iron candlesticks.

What Christianity has to offer is a bunch of ancient stuff that's about searching and exploration of the divine. What a gift we can give these students! Ancient spiritual practices that have

A RICH DIVERSITY

been proven over the centuries to foster a deeper relationship with the Creator of the universe. What could be better? Ancient spiritual disciplines, when rightly administered, have the ability to enfold an adolescent in God's love while fulfilling her desire for spiritual exploration.

The spiritual practices of the Christian tradition developed as individuals and communities moved along this spiritual journey, seeking greater communion with the Lord. Common to all practices in all traditions are prayer and Scripture, the two hallmarks of Christian spirituality. Other than that, the practices vary widely, heavily influenced by the people and times in which they were forged.

Of course, the divisions within the Christian church are mainly tragic, divisions that many today are trying to repair. But the splits between East and West in 1054 and between Protestant and Roman Catholic in 1517 have also led to a rich diversity in the field of spirituality. Each tradition has developed its own practices, and every practice carries the fingerprint of the milieu in which it was conceived. While some of these disciplines were virtually unknown across denominational lines for centuries, we live in a time of unprecedented cross-pollination.

The Roman Catholic Church places much emphasis on liturgy and the sacraments. For this reason, practices like the Stations of the Cross developed as a part of the sacrament of confession, and the Daily Office is, at its heart, a way to order the day liturgically. Even the labyrinth, as it was originally conceived, was to be walked as preparation for receiving the Eucharist. The Catholic Church also boasts John Cassian and Benedict of Nursia, the two men most responsible for the worldwide development of monasteries and, consequently, the disciplines that began therein.

The Orthodox Church is known to us most specifically in its Greek, Russian, and Antiochian forms. Those all share a spiritual tradition of *hesychasm* (from the Greek word for 'quietness'). The hesychasts, dating back to the fourth century, are monks who have taught that the way to enter God's Divine Light is prayer of absolute quiet, in which the heart and the mind become one. Centering Prayer and the Jesus Prayer are two examples of this type of prayer. Orthodox spirituality also relies heavily upon praying with icons, a tradition that is quite unfamiliar to most Western Christians.

Protestantism, the latest movement on the scene, has two distinct streams within it. Mainline Protestant spirituality is a roll-up-your-sleeves spirituality, with much emphasis on action, social justice, and bringing about the Kingdom of God on earth. Evangelical spirituality is guided more by personal Bible study and devotion, free-form prayer, and personal conversion to and relationship with Jesus.

All three of these traditions have added significantly to the depth and breadth of spiritual practices available to Christians. Indeed, a well-rounded believer of any denomination could do worse than committing to practice one discipline from each tradition.

THE PRACTICE

In a letter to the church in Corinth, the Apostle Paul used a metaphor to describe the Christian life:

Do you not know that in a race the runners all compete, but only one receives the prize? Run in such a way that you may win it. Athletes exercise self-control in all things; they do it to receive a perishable wreath, but we an imperishable one. So I do not run aimlessly, nor do I box as though beating the air; but I punish my body and enslave it, so that after proclaiming to others I myself should not be disqualified. [1 Corinthians 9:24-27 NRSV]

Ever since, athletic imagery has been common in describing the pursuit of a life with God. In English, words like *discipline*, *practice*, and *exercise* are common. In Greek, the word is *askesis* (as-kée-sis), translated 'exercise', or 'training'. Asceticism was common among the ancient Greek moral philosophers who encouraged moral training by avoiding fleshly pleasures; a similar concept is a guiding force in the wisdom literature of the Old Testament. When comparing the daily life of a Christian to carrying a cross, Jesus launched ascetical theology, and Paul wrote often about the need to be disciplined in the Christian life.

There are two sides to the coin of asceticism. On the negative side is self-abnegation—the discipline to practice restraint, moderation, and self-denial. Gregory of Sinai (d. 1360), a Desert Father, gives voice to this emphasis:

One thing more I have to add from my own experience: a monk can in no way succeed without the following virtues: fasting, abstinence, vigil, patience, courage, silence, prayer, not talking, tears, humility, which generate and preserve one another. Constant fasting withers lust, and gives birth to abstinence; abstinence to vigil; vigil to patience; patience to courage; courage to silence; silence to prayer; prayer to abstinence from talk; abstinence from talk to weeping; weeping to humility; humility again to weeping, and so on. [Kadloubovsky 92]

Ascetic disciplines have been commonly practiced in the church since the early centuries. Orders of monks were gathered around vows of celibacy and poverty, and the Desert Fathers and Mothers often practiced silence and fasting. Particularly in the Eastern church, this is related to Apophatic, or Negative Theology, the idea that any human conceptions of God (including language) are inadequate. Thus, the only way we can really achieve union with God is by ceasing all concep-

ASCETICAL YOUTH WORKERS

tions and all language, and only then approaching God in emptiness (silence, fasting, etc.).

The positive side of the asceticism coin is following Christ—striving after him. It's this action that Paul reminds us of when he uses athletic imagery. While an athlete may prepare for a race by refraining from fatty foods, alcohol, and late nights, eventually the race comes and the athlete must take the initiative to leave the starting blocks and run the course.

Christian writer Kathleen Norris writes, "Asceticism reminds us that our time, and our bodies, are not truly our own....The command comes out loud and clear: *be here, now*. And the demands of the body, the whining of the self, recede into the background." [Norris (1998) 362, 365] In other words, disciplining the body and the mind by way of spiritual practices aids us in focusing on *what really matters* in life: being loved by God…serving God…serving others.

To be blunt, many youth workers need the kind of discipline that has been practiced by the saints for centuries. For all of our good works and great ministry, a lot of youth workers are overworked and overweight, lacking discipline in patterns of eating, sleep, and study. Our churches can take some of the blame, for they seem to like youth workers who live somewhat out-of-control and boundary-less lives. But an undisciplined life is no way to live a life of ministry.

Beth Slevcove of Youth Specialties has spent time with more than 200 youth workers in the past few years. She loves youth workers and sees many positive trends in youth ministry, but she has also noticed some disheartening trends:

→ Instead of nurturing a spiritual intimacy with the Lord, many youth workers display compulsiveness to do more, work harder, and be better. This inevitably leads to exhaustion and despair.

→ Many are becoming aware *for the first time* that intimacy with Christ, a sense of being deeply loved, and a lasting peace are even possible.

→ Often there is a belief that youth workers should be strong enough Christians to do it all on their own and that sharing or asking for help is weakness.

→ Their prayer life tends to be more focused on talking and initiating than listening, receiving, responding.

→ Many lack a safe place to wrestle with issues, a safe person to be honest and accountable with.

→ Many are striving to live up to the stereotypical fun, charismatic, extroverted, cool youth worker, instead of recognizing their own giftedness and ministering in their own unique way.

→ Most have little sense of the importance of taking a sabbath in one form or another. They are forgetting that resting in God is required of us—constant productivity is not. ("When we have found our rest in God, we can do nothing other than minister," said Henri Nouwen.)

→ Many carry the false belief, *Who I Am = What I Do.*

→ Many have painfully expressed that they are living a kind of hypocrisy (due to a sin area, some crisis of faith, doubts, a recent or past deep wounding), but don't know any way out. This leads to hopelessness and feeling trapped.

Here's the good news: there is a solution! There is an imperishable wreath awaiting us, if we can exercise self-control and practice with determination. It takes strength and discipline, but the result will be ministering from a position of strength and intimacy with Christ. It's my hope that the ancient spiritual practices herein will help you find that place of strength and intimacy, and that your ministry will greatly benefit as a result.

It will not be easy. The history of the church is a story of many faithful Christians admirably fighting back their own sins by these disciplines, only to be thwarted again. But, as with a sport, the more you practice, the better you get. You'll get in better "spiritual shape" as you practice, and you'll be able to run the race to completion…even "in such a way that you may win it!"

Ironically, while athletic practice makes us stronger, physically and mentally, so that we're more present during a competition, spiritual discipline means making less of ourselves so that we can be more aware of what God is up to. Henri Nouwen said,

In the spiritual life, the word 'discipline' means "the effort to create some space in which God can act." Discipline means to prevent everything in your life from being filled up. Discipline means that somewhere you're not occupied, and certainly not preoccupied. In the spiritual life, discipline means to create that space in which something can happen that you hadn't planned or counted on. [Nouwen (1995)]

Part II: Via Contemplativa
Contemplative Approaches to Spirituality

Chapter 03

Sacred Reading

Do not read to satisfy curiosity or to pass the time, but study such things as move your heart to devotion.

Thomas à Kempis

A friend of mine was struggling with his profession, or at least his current work environment. He'd been attracted to this company when he did some consulting work for them and was recruited to come on board full time. But after a few years in the corporation, he began to see what an unhealthy and dysfunctional environment it was—the CEO was hostile and abusive, and the vast majority of the employees let him get away with it. But Peter was being paid well, they kept him busy, and he avoided the CEO as much as possible.

Not long ago, he was in Las Vegas to train a group of employees how to sell the line of products he had designed. Between the dysfunction of the organization and the rampant sin evident in downtown Vegas, Peter began to feel overwhelmed by grief. Heartsick, he rented a car and drove to Los Angeles to see some friends for the weekend. But instead of being his usual perky self, he holed up in a bedroom and lay on the bed, halfway between waking and sleeping. He drove back to Vegas Sunday night, dreading his Monday morning meeting with the CEO. In his hotel room that night, he opened his Bible. He'd been reading Paul of late, so he decided to turn to Jesus for help.

"I didn't even know where the Sermon on the Mount was," Peter told me recently, "But I looked around until I found it." That night, in the Embassy Suites in downtown Las Vegas, Peter read the fifth, sixth, and seventh chapters of St. Matthew's Gospel over and over. The more he read, the more two sections stuck out to him: Jesus' admonition to not worry (Matthew 6:25-34) and Jesus' exhortation to ask, seek, and knock (Matthew 7:7-11). "Something in me broke," Peter said, "I went from feeling like a caged animal to having everything become slow and peaceful—I think I finally abandoned my life to Christ that night."

On Monday morning he called his wife and told her he was quitting. She wholeheartedly agreed with his decision, and Peter went into the meeting with his boss with the boldness of true faith. (His job now is working to make the Internet a more powerful tool for youth ministry.)

This is *lectio divina*. *Lectio* (pronounced léx-ee-o) means reading, and *divina* (dih-vee-nah) means 'holy' or 'sacred'. Peter read the words of Christ with no agenda, with no predispositions (except despair of his current situation and faith that God speaks through holy Scripture). He came to the Bible naked, so

HISTORY

to speak, and let himself be clothed by God's Word. He came neither as a Bible scholar nor a teacher getting ready for a lesson; he didn't have to stop every two verses and answer questions in a study guide. No, he read the Bible as a sacred object, as an alive and dynamic revelation of God to *him*. And he read a complete section repeatedly and slowly, waiting for the revelation to be made known.

And indeed, God spoke to Peter that night.

Little did Peter know that in his hotel room that night he was engaging in a method of reading Scripture that innumerable monks have used in their caves, cells, cloisters, and sanctuaries since the earliest days of the church.

For the Israelites and the earliest Christians alike, the Psalter was their songbook. The 150 psalms that make up that book were their primary prayers, meditations, and pleas to God. As the New Testament was being compiled and immediately after, many different "senses" of Scripture reading were developed and articulated (see Theology section, page 39), and one of them was the meditative/devotional use of the Bible.

While the Desert Fathers and other early church leaders used the Scripture for their devotions, it was St. Benedict (c.480-c.550) who cemented the practice in Western monasticism. Born in Nursia, Italy, Benedict went to school in Rome. Disgusted with the sin of that city, he retreated to a village called Subaico in the hills. Once there, his reputation spread, and small bands of followers began to live with him. He organized them into monasteries of 12 brothers, each led by a spiritual Father (Abbot)—sound familiar? Around 529, many of them left Subaico and built a monastery at Monte Cassino (you can still see it from the *autostrada* between Rome and Naples), and around 540, Benedict wrote the *Rule of St. Benedict*. In the Rule, Benedict outlines life in a monastery—everything from the seven worship services per day to how to do the dishes.

The three elements that guide the life of a Benedictine monk are prayer, work, and *lectio divina*. The big difference between Benedict and many of the other early monastics was that he had little patience for solitaries and hermits—for Benedict, the Rule had to be lived out in community. And because of their dedication to holy reading, both of Scripture and of the other great texts of early Christianity, Benedictine monasteries are responsible for safeguarding much of the great literature of the world during the Dark Ages.

To understand the primacy that reading had in the life of a Benedictine monastery, we might remember what we learned in high school history class about the Dark Ages. Literacy was not common—often only clerics and royalty in a village could read. And books were scarce and exorbitantly expensive. As Benedict describes a day in the monastery, a significant portion of the day is spent reading—mainly monks individually reading books in a common room. Reading aloud is also a part of every day, at worship and at meals.

Lectio divina was articulated further by Guigo II (c.1115 - c.1198), the ninth prior of the Grand Chartreuse, a Carthusian order in France. In his book *Scala Claustralium* (*The Ladder of Monastics*), Guigo writes,

One day I was engaged in physical work with my hands and I began to think about the spiritual tasks we humans have. While I was thinking, four spiritual steps came to mind: reading (*lectio*), meditation (*meditatio*), prayer (*oratio*), and contemplation (*contemplatio*). This is the ladder of monastics by which they are lifted up from the earth into heaven. There are only a few distinct steps, but the distance covered is beyond measure and belief since the lower part is fixed on the earth and its top passes through the clouds to lay bare the secrets of heaven. [Casey 59]

These four steps have been foundational in the practice of the *lectio divina* ever since. Presently, sacred reading is still practiced in Benedictine and similar orders, and, across Christianity, it has become a popular method of approaching Scripture in our information-saturated world.

THEOLOGY

As mentioned above, the Psalter was the song/prayer book of Judaism and it continues to play that role today for both Jews and Christians. But in the years since Jesus, several ways of approaching Scripture have emerged. Immediately after the writing and distribution of the gospels and epistles, the early fathers had to go into a defensive mode against those attacking the unity of the Bible. Heretics like Marcion (d.c.160) questioned the inspiration of the entire Old Testament and much of the New Testament. Similar to the debates today between orthodox biblical scholars and the Jesus Seminar, the fathers had to develop scholarly credible means to defend the *literal* authenticity of Scripture.

At the time of the Reformation, Martin Luther and John Calvin advanced a Christocentric reading of Scripture, which has heavily influenced Protestant interpretation ever since. And following the scientific revolution of the Enlightenment, linguistic, historical-critical, text-critical, and redaction methods of interpretation, developed primarily in 19th century Germany, have held sway in some Protestant camps.

The Early Church Fathers utilized another Jewish method of reading the text, the *allegorical* method. In the ancient Greek and Hebrew tradition of allegory, a deeper meaning is hidden below the literal meaning of a passage—reading the lovers' story in the Song of Solomon as an allegory for the relationship between Israel and God is an example of this type of interpretation. In the Patristic period, the allegorical method was very popular, sometimes leading to highly dubious interpretations and even numerology. The allegorical method fell into disrepute in the wake of the Enlightenment.

In addition to the literal/historical and allegorical means of interpreting Scripture, a third method is finding the *moral* meaning of a text. By this method, the believer attempts to find application of the passage to her life and/or to her community of faith.

And finally, we come to a method of reading Scripture that inspires *lectio divina*: the *devotional* use of the Bible. One approaches the Bible devotionally believing that it's God's inspired Word—a living and active text with something to say to every believer. Few Christians would argue with reading the Bible devotionally; in fact, this is probably how most Christians, and particularly most middle and high school students, approach Scripture.

Lectio divina assumes that by entering deeply into the text of God's holy Word, God will be made known to us, speak to us, and direct our lives. Indeed, Paul's teaching that God's Word is "inspired" and "profitable" assumes that it is approachable by the average Christian. We need neither years of study nor thorough knowledge of both testaments to profit from *lectio*. As God's penultimate revelation to humankind (Jesus Christ being the ultimate revelation), holy Scripture is applicable to our lives and is the primary sourcebook for our devotion to God.

PRACTICE

Kathleen Norris has written of *lectio divina*: "It is not a method, but rather a type of free-form, serious play." [Norris (1998) 277-278] To keep this in mind is of ultimate importance when developing a practice of sacred reading.

The initial preparation for practicing *lectio* is to purposefully shed the common methods of reading of our day. The fact is, we read mostly for entertainment and information. Whether it be a novel, the newspaper, magazines, professional journals, or the Bible, we read almost exclusively for these two reasons, and so do the kids with whom we work. We need to approach the Bible differently for *lectio*. This is harder than it sounds, particularly for those of us trained in Bible study, either formally or informally.

First it means finding a Bible that's easily readable, without distracting notes and boxed-out "life applications." We should use a version that uses poetic form for the poetry and paragraph form for the prose. For this reason, many suggest the *New Jerusalem Bible* for accuracy of translation, not only in the words, but also in the rhythms and form of the Hebrew and Greek originals. Eugene Peterson's paraphrase, *The Message*, is also excellent for *lectio*. Avoid using a Bible that has marks, underlinings, and notes from past reading and study—they can distract you from what God is saying to you *today*.

Secondly, attend to the surroundings. *Lectio divina* requires quiet, even silence. Have enough light to read, but not so much as to be distracting. Choose a time of day when you're wide awake, and neither too hungry nor too full to concentrate. Obviously, turn off the cell phone and any other external distractions. And block out enough time to hear from God.

Thirdly, choose a text on which to meditate. Being inspired, the entirety of Scripture is able to be digested through *lectio*—but many parts are difficult to meditate on except for the most experienced reader. Better for the beginner to choose from a more obvious source of devotion: a psalm, the epistles of John, Ecclesiastes, or any part of the Gospels.

Many people like to begin *lectio* with a prayer requesting—indeed, expecting—God's presence and direction. Others like to read the same section of the same psalm every day to begin; Psalm 119 lends itself to this with its praise of God's Word.

Now, let's use the rungs of Guigo II's ladder to guide us in *lectio divina*:

Lectio: Having chosen the passage on which you are going to meditate and situating yourself in a spot that's conducive to sacred reading, set about reading the section of Scripture slowly, repeatedly, and aloud if possible. Michael Casey calls this *active reading:* "we need to slow down, to savor what we read, and to allow the text to trigger memories and associations that reside below the threshold of awareness." [Casey 83] This isn't the rapid reading of the morning paper or an e-mail; it's calm, deliberate, and gradual. I like to imagine what my temperament will be in heaven, sitting at God's feet, listening, and being instructed. I don't imagine I'll be shifting in my seat, my hand up to ask a question. I imagine I'll be content, calm, and listening hard for what God has to say to *me*. What I often find is that a certain word or phrase rises above the rest of the text and grabs a hold of me.

Meditatio (med-i-tá-tsee-o): Guigo calls this step the "interior intelligence" of the text. That is, what are the values, the underlying assumptions and presumptions of this passage? As you attend to those deeper meanings, begin to meditate on the feelings and emotions that are conjured in your inner self. Different texts will evoke joy, sorrow, satisfaction, barrenness—and different individuals will experience different emotions in the same text.

Today, in a group lectio, we read and heard the passage Isaiah 43:1-2:

"But now thus says the LORD, he who created you, O Jacob, he who formed you, O Israel: Do not fear, for I have redeemed you; I have called you by name, you are mine. When you pass through the waters, I will be with you; and through the rivers, they shall not overwhelm you; when you walk through fire you shall not be burned, and the flame shall not consume you."

What I heard over and over was, "I have redeemed you." I focused, thought, prayed, and listened. Of that phrase, the word *redeemed* kept coming up, and I really tried to think about what redeemed means in its theological sense, and what it means to me personally.

While that was fruitful, far more powerful was just letting the phrase, "I have redeemed you" wash over me. That's probably the best way I can describe it—washing over me like a kind of baptism. I took a long walk and, in my mind, repeated the phrase over and over, dozens of times, one word per step: I...have...redeemed...you... It was a long and deliberate walk. I couldn't go very quickly since I was repeating these words. But it was awesome. It was like, by the end, I truly felt redeemed—like, I actually believe that he redeemed me!!!

Oratio (o-rá-tsee-o): Although the *lectio* is covered in prayer from beginning to end, and, indeed, the entire exercise can be seen as a prayer, Guigo emphasizes that the next rung in the ladder is to deliberately ask God for illumination. Again, this is an active step in *lectio*, conversing with God about the meaning of the emotions that are being experienced.

Contemplatio (con-tem-plá-tsee-o): The final step is the most difficult to describe and the most difficult to achieve. True contemplation moves beyond words and intellect and into that "thin space" where time and eternity almost touch. It's in moments like these that some of the greatest saints in the history of the church have had a "mystical union" with Christ. That is not to say that contemplation is unavailable to you and me, just that it takes patience and practice. So don't get discouraged if your first attempts at contemplation seem unfulfilling.

Of these four steps, Guigo writes,

From what has been said we may gather that reading without meditation is dry. Meditation without reading is subject to error. Prayer without meditation is lukewarm. Meditation without prayer is fruitless. Prayer with devotion leads to contemplation whereas contemplation without prayer happens rarely or by a miracle. [Casey 62]

Let's look at two variations of the traditional *lectio*:

Group Lectio: Especially popular in places where books are scarce, the practice of *lectio* can be a fantastic experience for a group, and it's gaining popularity in churches across North America. Although the form can vary widely, it might look something like this: after an opening prayer, the passage is read two or three times, slowly and deliberately, and participants are asked to mull over the word or phrase silently that speaks to them. After sharing that word with the others in their groups, the passage is read again, two or three times, with a different voice (different gender, or two or three in unison). Again, in silence, participants reflect on the word or phrase that speaks to them, this time attending to the emotions or feelings that it conjures. Finally, after sharing within small groups, the passage is read twice more in distinct voices and a longer period of silence is kept to ask God why this word and this feeling have been provoked. A final and more lengthy time of sharing ends the session, with each person telling the small group what God seems to be saying through the text.

Reading Nonbiblical Texts: St. Francis de Sales (1567-1622), a founder of the Modern Devotion movement, wrote, "There is no more difference between the Gospel written and the life of a saint than between music written and music sung." Any Christian who has spent time reading some of the classics of Christian devotion (e.g., St. Augustine's *Confessions*, Thomas à Kempis' *Imitation of Christ*, St. John of the Cross' *The Ladder of Divine Ascent*) probably agrees with him. While all Christians hold the Bible as the inspired Word of God, and therefore the primary source of *lectio divina*, many of the great works of Christian faith can likewise lead us into deep devotion. If this kind of reading is new to you, experiment—you'll probably find an author or two in the Christian tradition with whom you particularly resonate.

THOUGHTS FOR YOUTH MINISTRY

Lectio divina is one of the ancient spiritual practices that I've used most in our youth ministry. Students have responded to it very favorably, finding it brings the Bible to life, resurrecting what some had considered a dead, boring, and irrelevant book. That sounds pretty strong, I know, but even though our kids say they know the Bible and they trust the Bible, the fact is it's pretty lifeless to a lot of them. We've too often misused Scripture as a kind of proof-texting source or a source of morals (a friend of mine calls our proclivity to find a moral at the end of every biblical story the "Aesop's Fable-ization of the Bible").

Serious Bible study—working with the literal, allegorical, and moral senses of Scripture—will always be a part of good youth ministry. But giving students a practice through which they can approach the Bible devotionally, we not only add to the angles by which they can come at God's Word, we give them a method of reading that often results in this *living* Word giving them *life*. Imagine your students going off to college, cherishing the Bible because of how God has spoken through it into their lives. In fact, if they practice it enough, they may head off to college with a *florilegium* (floor-i-lég-ium), a book of the collected verses that have spoken to them over the years.

A FINAL WORD

Guigo gets the last word on *lectio*:

Reading is an exterior exercise; meditation belongs to the inner intellect. Prayer operates at the level of desire. Contemplation transcends every sense. Reading is proper to beginners, meditation to proficients, prayer to those with devotion, and contemplation to the blessed. [Casey 60-61]

Chapter 04

Silence and Solitude

In silence and quietness the devout soul makes progress and learns the hidden mysteries of the Scriptures.

Thomas à Kempis

Mo Shields works for YouthFront, a youth ministry organization in Kansas City. She writes:

And then there was…silence?

It's hard to believe, but there it was. A couple weeks ago my discipleship group, LILINI, did its first ever silent retreat. We met at 8:30 on Saturday morning, loaded up our cars with books, Bibles, journals, pillows, sleeping bags, and munchies, and headed out to Circle-C Camp to be quiet. I was surprised by how excited the girls were to do this; I mean, I knew that I enjoyed the chance to get away and spend some time alone and in silence with God, but I didn't know if they would like it.

They did. We spent seven hours at Circle-C. Each girl had her own room so she wasn't distracted. I told them they could read, they could draw, they could even sleep, or they could go for a walk around camp—what they couldn't do was listen to music on their portable CD players, do homework, or talk to each other.

What an experience it is to be with eight high school girls for seven hours and not hear a peep out of them. Wow. God used that day to teach each of them differently, and that was great to see. One comment that struck me was, "I kind of think it was too short. I wish we could have stayed here for 24 hours."

Silence, solitude, being still before God—students *can* do it!

Becky is one of the students in Mo's group:

Can you even imagine being quiet for seven hours? Well, I sure couldn't. But when I got to Circle-C, my attitude changed. I spent most of my time outside, walking around the lake and through the woods. It was amazing. Amazingly beautiful, amazingly peaceful, and amazingly quiet. I talked to God. And I talked to him. And prayed to him. And I even sang to him.

It was such a wonderful experience for me, just being with God, no distractions. Just seeing nature and the beautiful things he created.

Anyway, I have to wrap this up pretty soon, so I'll just tell you one more thing about the silent retreat. If you've never been on one, you should seriously consider going on one. Being quiet for a *really* long time may sound hard, but it's worth it.

HISTORY

"The tongue has the power of life and death, and those who love it will eat its fruit." So says the wise author of Proverbs [18:21], and many places within the Old and New Testaments stand in agreement. Ancient philosophers of all stripes agree—their consensus is that to speak much is a vice, and to keep silent is a virtue. While Jesus did teach, he also valued his times of silence and solitude, seeking them for prayer, reflection, and at times of distress. And *The Catholic Encyclopedia* emphatically states, "All writers on the spiritual life uniformly recommend, nay, command under penalty of total failure, the practice of silence." [www.newadvent.org]

All in all, no spiritual discipline is more universally acclaimed as necessary than the practice of silence. The Desert Fathers retreated to the wild lands of Egypt; Rufinus (c. 345-411), who toured the desert to visit as many of the Fathers as he could, wrote to Jerome, "This is the utter desert where each monk remains alone in his cell…. There is a huge silence and a great quiet here." [Ward 3] In fact, as more and more pilgrims like Rufinus crowded the desert to pester the Fathers, the desert monks withdrew into deeper parts of the wilderness to find the quiet they desired.

Likewise, Benedict fashioned much of his *Rule* around the keeping of silence. When talking is allowed, it's to be done with charity and moderation, and useless and idle words are always forbidden. Areas of the monastery exist where talking is necessary and permitted, but in other areas and at certain times of the day, silence is strictly observed. And after Compline, the Great Silence is kept until prayers the next morning.

Present day spiritual writers commend silence as well. Richard Foster carries on the tradition, linking silence and solitude: "Without silence there is no solitude. Though silence sometimes involves the absence of speech, it always involves the act of listening. Simply to refrain from talking, without a heart listening to God, is not silence." [Foster 98]

Ultimately, we keep silence and solitude so that we can listen better—so that we can hear what God is saying, to us and to our world. It's like when we're on the phone with a friend who has something important to tell us, and we move out of the noisy room with the TV on and the vacuum running and shut ourselves in a closet so that we can really hear what our friend is saying. That's the kind of attentive listening that silence and solitude engenders.

THEOLOGY

The tradition that Foster continues, coupling solitude and silence, goes back at least to Jesus. In preparation for his ministry, Jesus spent 40 days in the wilderness outside of Jerusalem, setting the example for the monks who would follow him there three centuries later. Clearly in solitude, Jesus was presumably in silence as well, talking only to his *Abba*, 'father'—and, finally, rebuffing Satan.

From then on, Jesus made a habit of withdrawing to "the hills" or "a lonely place" or "the wilderness" or "a high mountain" or the Garden of Gethsemene. He went there before he chose his 12 disciples, after he heard of his cousin John's beheading, after feeding the 5,000, after healing a leper, before the transfiguration, and, of course, to prepare for his passion. "The seeking out of solitary places was a regular practice for Jesus. So it should be for us." [Foster 97]

But what do silence and solitude accomplish in us? When I informally poll the students I work with, I find that most of them have no silence and little solitude in their lives. They are awakened by a clock radio, eat breakfast to morning television, drive to school with music, talk in the halls to friends, listen to teachers, wear headphones during passing time, listen to music on the way home, have the TV on while they IM friends after school, eat dinner with the TV on, do homework with headphones on, and fall asleep with music playing. Theirs is a life filled with noise.

I also listen to many students in my office (so many it's baffling) who feel depressed or are even suffering from diagnosed clinical depression. Many factors contribute to this, but one fact is noticeable: all the noise and all the talking does not quell the major symptom of this depression—loneliness. Although these students are surrounded by the stimuli of music, television, and conversation (both personal and virtual), they feel disconnected from other people, from God, and, ultimately, from themselves.

Spiritual writers, ancient and modern, are unanimous in saying that silence and solitude lead to a love of God, a love of self, and a love of others. In the 430s, Abba Arsenius lived in the desert. Prior to this, while living in a palace, he asked God how he could be led in the way of salvation, and a voice answered him, "Arsenius, flee from men and you will be saved." Once in the desert, he prayed the same prayer and this time he heard, "Arsenius, flee, be silent, pray always, for these are the source of sinlessness." [Ward 8]

The reason a Christian seeks silence and solitude first of all is the same reason Jesus did: to be able to hear from God. John Climacus (c.570-c.649), a Desert Father, wrote in his classic *The Ladder of Divine Ascent*, "The lover of silence draws close to God. He talks to him in secret and God enlightens him." [Mack 61] Humble silence opens the ears and causes the listener to hear that "sound of sheer silence" [1 Kings 19:12 NRSV] with which God so often speaks.

The second reason to practice silence and solitude is to find what we can learn from ourselves when we turn off the external stimuli that are so much a part of our world. But that silence often leads to what one medieval writer, St. John of the Cross (1542-1591), called *The Dark Night of the Soul*. It seems one cannot pursue true silence without, rather quickly, coming to this deep, dark doubt. Twentieth century monk Thomas Merton (1915-1968) talks about this experience in a passage that deserves to be quoted in full:

The hermit, all day and all night, beats his head against a wall of doubt. That is his contemplation. Do not mistake my meaning. It is not a question of intellectual doubt, an analytical investigation of theological, philosophical, or some other truths. It is something else, a kind of unknowing of his own self, a kind of doubt which undermines his very reasons for existing and for doing what he does. It is this doubt which reduces him finally to silence, and in the silence which ceases to ask questions, he receives the only certitude he knows: the presence of God in the midst of uncertainty and nothingness, as the only reality....

Beyond and in all this, he possesses his solitude, the riches of his emptiness his interior poverty: but of course, it is not a possession. It is an established fact. It is there. It is assured. In fact, it is inescapable. It is everything—his whole life. It contains God, surrounds him with God, plunges him in God. [Merton (1977) 206-7]

Each of us probably desires and fears, in equal measure, being plunged into God. For there we must confront our deadliest sins and deepest doubts. But there, as Merton writes a few pages later, when we enter into the loneliness of the God who emptied himself on our behalf, "is a joy beyond human comment and appreciation. About such joy nothing can be said. Silence alone can worthily express it." [Merton (1977) 210] We emerge from the dark night of the soul, if we have the patience and fortitude to endure it, stronger and more faithful.

This is the best, right now. I'm at the cabin, it's 5 a.m., everyone else is asleep. We're near the summer solstice, so the days are long. The sun is just coming up over the swamp, there's a little breeze, and all I can hear are leaves, birds, and the coffeemaker chugging out its brew. I'll sit on the deck, look at the lake, and let the sun rise up over my back until I hear those little voices in the baby monitor. What will I do during this time? The possibilities are many and thrilling—the Jesus Prayer, Centering Prayer, consolations and desolations, maybe a combination of several. It's so much easier to get out of bed up here, even if I stayed up too late last night. Soli Deo Gloria!

Friday morning, it wasn't so easy to keep silence. I was the only one up here, and it was more lonely than silent when I got up. First thing I turned on NPR for the news and the companionship. But I knew silence was better for me, like broccoli, so I turned off the radio and started to listen. It was good.

For we find our true selves when we're swallowed up in God. We discover our true identity, not as *do-ers*, but as *be-ers*. Our tasks in this life boil down to: "Be still, and know that I am God." [Psalm 46:10] Indeed, this is why many of us avoid silence and solitude, because our self-identities are bound up in our busyness. We're consumed with managing our ministries, maintaining friendships, and loving our families. And we're doing all of this in an effort to love God, to do God's will (to *earn* our salvation?!). But back in the recesses of our minds, we know that if we slow down long enough, and be quiet long enough, all these things, tasks, events, do-ings, will recede in importance. Where will we find our identities? Although it's a scary prospect to lose the things that give us meaning, the spiritual masters promise that we'll find, in our silence, a meaning more profound than we could ever imagine.

Beyond this new self-identity, spiritual fruit results from silence and solitude. As John Climacus tells us, "Intelligent silence is the mother of prayer, freedom from bondage, custodian of zeal, a guard on our thoughts, a watch on our enemies…a companion of stillness, the opponent of dogmatism, a growth of knowledge, a hand to shape contemplation, hidden progress, the secret journey upward." [Mack 60] Ultimately, Richard Foster writes, "the fruit of solitude is increased sensitivity and compassion for others. There comes a new freedom to be with people. There is a new attentiveness to their needs, new responsiveness to their hurts." [Foster 108] In other words, being quiet and being alone make us better youth workers.

PRACTICE

I don't know about where you live, but where I live, silence takes an enormous amount of discipline, and solitude takes even more. I'd like to do it at 5:30 a.m., but my kids most often get up about then. I'd like to try silence, as many suggest, around Vespers time (late afternoon, before dinner), but my wife Julie calls those "the arsenic hours" with the kids. I'd like to do it at 9:00 p.m., reviewing the day, but that's the only time of the day that Julie gets to have adult conversation.

So, like many of the other practices, it has to get on the calendar. I try to schedule one half-day of silence per month, a two-day silent retreat per year, a week-long silent retreat every five years (that happens to line up with my sabbatical plan), and—God willing—a 30-day Ignatian retreat before I die.

It takes a while to enter into true silence, and it takes effort to find solitude, but it can be found. Maybe someone in your church has a lake home or a place in the mountains that they'd let you borrow. There is surely a monastery or convent nearby that would let you make retreat there. Be creative. Take your tent to a state park and camp out for a weekend. Bring a couple of the devotional classics commended in the back of this book. Try a few practices, read a little, take a nap, walk in nature.

At first the silence can be scary, lonely, oppressive. But most often it turns into joy and peace after a time.

THOUGHTS FOR YOUTH MINISTRY

We can follow Mo's example from the beginning of this chapter and offer silent retreats, one or two days long, to our students. We can also, on any of our retreats or camps, ask them to observe silence from the final chapel service of the night until breakfast the next morning. We can even take some students with us to the monastery when we go on our own annual silent retreat.

On a smaller scale, try a Wednesday night meeting in absolute silence. Don't talk about it when the students arrive—just put a sign up at the door that says "SILENCE" or "Silence is being observed tonight." If the room is dark with no music and the foosball table is pushed to the corner, they'll get the idea. Maybe have some material for journaling or artwork laid out. Have a few candles lit and an icon or two for meditation. At the end of the hour, stand up and give a benediction. That's it. Don't try to process or debrief the experience immediately—do that later, maybe the next week.

Of course, a night of silence like this will probably work better if you've already taught your students some contemplative practices, so don't try it this week. First, start with a practice of silence yourself, take your leaders on a silent retreat, and begin to develop the contemplative paradigm in your ministry. *Then* try a night of silence.

A FINAL WORD

Kathleen Norris, award-winning author of *The Cloister Walk*, used to teach art to elementary students in the Dakotas. She worked hard to get these rambunctious little ones to settle down and be quiet so that they could interact with art, so first she let them be loud and then she got them to be silent. Then she asked them to write about the noise and the silence.

What interests me most about my experiment is the way in which making silence liberated the imagination of so many children. Very few wrote with any originality about making noise. Most of their images were clichés such as "we sound like a herd of elephants." But silence was another matter: here, their images often had a depth and maturity that was unlike anything else they wrote. One boy came up with an image of strength being "as slow and silent as a tree," another wrote that "silence is me sleeping waiting to wake up. Silence is a tree spreading its branches to the sun." In a parochial school, one third grader's poem turned into a prayer: "Silence is spiders spinning their webs, it's like a silkworm making its silk. Lord, help me know when to be silent." And in a tiny town in western North Dakota a little girl offered a gem of spiritual wisdom I find myself returning to when my life becomes too noisy and distractions overwhelm me: "Silence reminds me to take my soul with me wherever I go." [Norris (1998) 17]

And Henri Nouwen has some good words for those of us in ministry:

"As ministers our greatest temptation is toward too many words. They weaken our faith and make us lukewarm. But silence is a sacred discipline, a guard of the Holy Spirit." [Nouwen (1981) 40]

Chapter 05
The Jesus Prayer

Let all your thoughts be with the Most High, and direct your humble prayers unceasingly to Christ.

Thomas à Kempis

Sometime in the middle of the 19th century, a young man in his 20s set out on a quest. His wife had just died, and his right hand was withered from a childhood accident, making it uncommonly difficult for him to find work. He began to wander the countryside of his native Russia. He was embarking on a quest because he had recently heard in church the Apostle Paul's exhortations to "pray without ceasing," [1 Thessalonians 5:17 NRSV] "pray in the Spirit on all occasions," [Ephesians 6:18] and "I want men everywhere to lift up holy hands in prayer," [1 Timothy 2:8], and he wanted to know if this was truly possible.

Taking this biblical appeal more seriously than one might expect, he walked from town to town, seeking out priests, monks, and other wise elders who might help him answer this question. One day while walking along a country road, a man in monk's clothes came walking alongside him. The young man posed to him the question of his quest: "Is unceasing prayer possible?" The old monk answered that indeed, it is possible to continually pray, and he invited the young man back to his monastery, only a few miles up the road, to learn more about this.

As they approached the hermitage, the old man explained that true ceaseless prayer comes in quieting the mind and making the mind one with the heart. As they entered the old man's cell, the young man was about to burst: "Please, be gracious, Reverend Father, and explain the meaning of ceaseless mental prayer to me and show me how I can learn to practice it!"

As they entered his cell, the old hermit explained, "The ceaseless Jesus Prayer is a continuous, uninterrupted call on the holy name of Jesus Christ with the lips, mind and heart; and in the awareness of His abiding presence it is a plea for His blessing in all undertakings, in all places, at all times, even in sleep. The words of the Prayer are: 'Lord Jesus Christ, have mercy on me.' Anyone who becomes accustomed to this Prayer will experience great comfort as well as the need to say it continuously. He will become accustomed to it to such a degree that he will not be able to do without it and eventually the Prayer will flow in him." [Bacovin 20]

Then the old hermit handed the young pilgrim a book, the *Philokalia*, the collected works of the Desert Fathers, and pointed out to him the passages regarding the Jesus Prayer. The young man found a hut to live in about three miles away, and he spent a week studying the selections from the *Philokalia*.

Then he went back to the old monk and asked him to become his *starets*, his spiritual director. The old man agreed and told the young man to go back to his hut and recite the Prayer 3,000 times per day. He also gave the young man a prayer rope with 100 knots to keep track of the number of recitations.

Although the first two days were challenging, the young man soon found the Prayer to be easy and delightful. A week later, he returned to his *starets* and told him these things. The old man told him to increase the repetitions to 6,000 per day. Within 10 days, the young pilgrim had grown so accustomed to the Prayer that he felt as though something was missing when he wasn't saying it, and this he told to his *starets* at their next meeting. "Do not waste any time," the *starets* replied, "but decide, with the help of God, to recite the Prayer 12,000 times a day. Rise earlier and retire later; stay alone, and every two weeks come to me for direction." [Bacovin 22]

At first, the young man had great difficulty in following the hermit's direction. His tongue went numb and his jaw got tight. His thumb ached and his forearm swelled from working the rope. But as the days passed, the Prayer became the air that the pilgrim breathed; it woke him up in the morning, it overwhelmed him during the day, and he dreamed about it at night. Every recitation was pure joy, filling him with both emotional and physical light. He began to feel love for everyone he met, considering each his brother or sister.

Shortly thereafter, the young pilgrim's *starets* died and the pilgrim began once again to wander the Russian steppe country. He met many people along the way, many of whom he taught about the Prayer. On summer nights he slept under trees, and in winter he found for himself some kind of humble lodging. All the while, whether walking or resting, eating or sleeping, contemplating or working, he recited the Prayer, and the Prayer became one with him, reflecting his breath and his heartbeat.

The anonymous Russian pilgrim left us the story of his journeys and discoveries in the wonderful little book, *The Way of a Pilgrim*.

HISTORY

What the pilgrim happened upon in the 1850s has actually been a foundation of Eastern Christian spirituality since the fifth century. Following the age of the Apostles, those who knew and followed Jesus, was the age of the Martyrs. The many who lost their lives to Roman persecution were looked to by early Christians as saints worthy of remembrance and veneration. When the Emperor Constantine legalized and even promoted Christianity beginning in 313 and martyrs were no longer common, Christians began to look to the first monks for wisdom. The tradition of monasticism (from the Greek *monachus* meaning 'solitary person') began in the East where some men and women retreated from cities into the Egyptian and Syrian deserts. These people became known as the Desert Fathers and Mothers.

Their withdrawal from society was noteworthy, to be sure, but it was the teachings and writings from these desert dwellers that really began to attract some attention. Reports from the desert told of divine appearances, words from the Lord, and moments of mystical union with Christ. As these teachings circulated in both oral and written form, many city dwellers made pilgrimage to the desert to learn from the Fathers and Mothers.

Whereas in the West, the Patristic period (that of the Church Fathers) was considered to be over in the seventh century, in the East, the witness of the Fathers and Mothers is considered an ongoing one. Although earlier Fathers wrote about contemplative prayer invoking Jesus' name, the first to mention the Jesus Prayer was Abba Philemon of the sixth century. Since Abba Philemon, dozens of Eastern contemplatives and mystics have written about the Prayer, making it the centerpiece of Eastern Christian spirituality.

The Way of a Pilgrim continued that trend into the modern era, endorsing the Jesus Prayer in a compelling and winsome, albeit anonymous, narrative. The pilgrim's story revitalized interest in the Prayer and in Eastern spirituality, and, partly as a result, the *Philokalia* was translated into English for the first time in the 1950s.

THEOLOGY

Beginning with the teaching of Origen (c.185-254), Eastern theologians believed that body, mind, and spirit were so intimately intertwined that the soul could only truly commune with God If removed from all other distractions. Two emphases of the Eastern monastic movement have exerted influence since Origen and Gregory of Nyssa (c.330-c.395):

Asceticism (as-ké-ti-sizm). From the Greek word for 'training' or 'exercise,' asceticism follows from the teachings of Christ and Paul that Christians must deny themselves in order to follow Jesus. An ascetic, therefore, denies him- or herself many of the pleasures common to a life lived in society, like marriage, sex, property, and generous portions of food. While the negative side of asceticism is voluntary forfeiture of these pleasures, the positive side is the opportunity to follow Christ exclusively, without the external hindrances that these pleasures so often entail.

Hesychasm (héz-ee-kazm). From the Greek word for 'quietness,' the hesychasts believed that if the mind could achieve true silence, then it could hear from God. Actually, Eastern theology has less to do with the individual receiving a word or divine instruction from the Lord and more to do with mystically uniting with the Lord in his Divine Light. The way to do this, they

taught, was to unite the mind and the heart in prayer, known as "the Prayer of the Heart." When this is truly accomplished, through quieting the mind, focusing it on the heart, and repetitively praying a simple phrase, God's Light will illumine the believer, particularly to the truth of Scripture.

Although these are big Greek words, I mention them because they are so unfamiliar to those of us who were reared in the faith of the Western church. In fact, at first blush, we may completely disagree with both of these ideas—doesn't God desire us to be *in* but not *of* the world? What good are monks anyway? Isn't it just escapism to run off to the desert in order to commune with God?

Good questions, all. But we know how powerful retreats are, don't we? Some of the best youth ministry we do takes place *away* from the distractions of church and home. And we ourselves are fueled when we spend a time apart from friends, work, even family, to reconnect with God for a time. What these Desert Fathers and Mothers did was to extend the retreat over the course of 30 or 40 years in some cases, all the while sending correspondence back to the "real world"—though one might argue that the union with Christ they experienced was actually the *most* real world!

The result of retreat to the desert and what's variously called the Prayer of the Heart, mental prayer, or self-activating prayer, according to Gregory of Sinai (d.1360) is gradient:

To some there comes the spirit of fear, rending the mountains of passions and breaking in pieces on the rocks—hardened hearts—such fear that the flesh seems to be pierced by nails and numbed as in death. Others quake, being filled with joy—what the fathers called the leaping of joy. In yet others, preeminently in those who have achieved success in prayer, God produces a subtle and serene glow of light when Christ comes to dwell in the heart and to shine mysteriously in the spirit. [Kadloubovsky and Palmer 83]

Ultimately, some of the desert dwellers even experienced Christ's light in a more powerful and dramatic way, an experience that was often compared to the disciples' vision of Jesus, Moses, and Elijah on the Mount of Transfiguration (Matthew 17:1-8 and parallels).

Of course, the Prayer itself is strongly rooted in the Gospels, an amalgam of many who called out to Jesus, including blind Bartimaeus by the side of the road who shouted, "Jesus, son of David, have mercy on me," [Mark 10:47 (parallel, Luke 18:38)] and the tax collector in Jesus' parable who beat his breast and cried out, "God, have mercy on me, a sinner." [Luke 18:13] The cry for mercy, for God's unrelenting steadfast love, is a constant of Scripture, Old and New Testaments alike. The need for God's mercy seems obvious, upon reflection, but, Frederica Mathewes-Green writes,

The problem is not in God's willingness to have mercy, but in our forgetting that we need it. We keep lapsing into ideas of self-sufficiency, or get impressed with our niceness, and so we lose our humility. Asking for mercy reminds us that we are still poor and needy, and fall short of the glory of God. Those who do not ask do not receive, because they don't know their own need. [Mathewes-Green 73]

To cry out for mercy as a helpless sinner seems foreign to modern sensibilities, even to modern Christianity. All the more reason for us to make a practice of doing it.

PRACTICE

There is some variation in the actual form of the Prayer. The simple formulation, "Christ, have mercy on me," echoes the ancient cry of the church, *"Kyrie eleison, Christe eleison, Kyrie eleison* ('Lord, have mercy; Christ, have mercy; Lord, have mercy')." The fuller text of the Prayer combines the Scripture passages quoted above: *"Lord Jesus Christ, Son of God, have mercy on me, a sinner."*

While the final self-referential tag, "a sinner," seems like a harsh conclusion, it is, of course, the truth. Many modern recitations of the Prayer omit this ending, but I always use it in my own practice. It stings me and awakens me to my own weakness. It also makes the Prayer a loop, for as I conclude by considering my own sinfulness, I'm compelled to once again call upon God's mercy for my life. In this way, when practiced rhythmically, the Prayer has no beginning and no end.

The *Philokalia* is full of hundreds of pages of advice about practicing the Jesus Prayer. Among them are the instructions left by 14th-century monks Callistus and Ignatius, who were said to have left behind "full and perfect knowledge of the Jesus Prayer." [Kadloubovsky and Palmer 83] They recommend that a person be, firstly, "earnest and undistracted," and in a place of absolute silence—silence being the most important thing to guard, and it may be the most difficult for us to find in a modern world. For me this often means getting up early in the morning before the family rises (I am too prone to fall asleep late at night).

Callistus and Ignatius also recommend a "dimly lit room." While the Prayer can later be practiced outside in nature, in a public place, or even while driving, at first it's necessary to sequester oneself from all visual distractions as well. This way whether the eyes are open or shut, concentration can be focused solely on the Prayer.

Now that the external setting is taken care of, the most important aspect of preparation for the Prayer can take place. With great concentration, one can cause "the mind to descend into the heart with the breath." At first, this was a concept as foreign to me as it may be to you. However, with some practice, this method becomes a means of guarding the mind from diversions. In fact, many of the Fathers recommend that one bows the head and fixes the eyes on the place of the heart in order to facilitate this concentration.

The "place of the heart" is, obviously, the focus of the Prayer of

So it turns out that the whole reason to practice spiritual disciplines is to overcome my overwhelming proclivity to sin. (Of course, that's overstated—they also help us move closer to God and be more prepared to serve our fellow humans.) The more I fill my mind and body with the things of God, the less I'll be tempted to think about/act on the things that pull me away from God. What's amazing is how quickly my mind and my body move toward sin when I veer from the disciplines.

Everything in my American bloodstream, everything in my DirecTV, two-car-three-bedroom-one-and-three-quarter-bath DNA is repelled by the disciplines. Take for instance the Jesus Prayer—how boring! But I find such comfort in the routine, the simplicity. No more searching for how to guide my prayer. No more wondering what form to pray in. No more worrying that I hadn't spent enough time adoring or confessing or thanking or supplicating.

Last night I think I did pretty well. Of course, I floated in and out of concentration, but I worked really hard to be disciplined. If I caught myself fading, I moved right back into the prayer. For the first 30 minutes, I prayed the Jesus Prayer, and I think I found a breathing rhythm that will work for me: Breathing in: *Lord Jesus Christ, Son of the Living God*; breathing out: *Have mercy on me, a sinner*. Then I went online and prayed through the *sacredspace* prayer for the day. After that I took a break, ate a snack, drank some water, and walked around for a few minutes.

When I went back to the prayer room, I started through the Psalms. When I found my mind wandering, I'd switch translations—from the Message to the NRSV (on my Palm) to the BCP (also on the Palm). Finally, the alarm on my Palm went off at 1:45, and I prayed Compline. Then I went to bed.

the Heart. It's difficult for us to imagine the heart without thinking of pumps, paddles, hospitals, and bypasses. But remember,

In ancient times, before the interior of the body was charted, emotions were ascribed to sites throughout the torso: heart, kidneys, bowels, and womb. The spiritual heart is not the same as that general region of feeling or compassion. Nor is it merely the fleshy pump that beats in our chests. This heart is the spiritual center of a person's entire being. [Mathewes-Green 63]

So, seated comfortably in a dimly lit room with the head bowed, attend to your breathing, and then begin the prayer in rhythm with your breathing. Breathe in: "Lord Jesus Christ, Son of God"; breathe out: "have mercy on me, a sinner." Guarding the mind against all distractions, the pray-er focuses during every repetition on the meaning of the words, praying them from the heart and in the heart.

Since clocks were not a reality when the Prayer was first practiced, instead of designating an amount of time to pray, a number of repetitions was determined ahead of time. The pilgrim started at 3,000 repetitions per day—if the normal person takes between 12 and 15 breaths per minute, this takes between three and four hours. When the pilgrim got to 12,000 repetitions, it was taking him between 11 and 14 hours. That's probably out of reach for you and me, but 100 or 500 prayers is a valuable and achievable practice.

In order to keep track of my repetitions, I use a prayer rope (called a *chockti* in Slavonic and a *komvoschinon* in Greek). Most are made in a monasteries on Mt. Athos in Greece with 100 knots, each knot tied with nine crosses (though they also come with 33, 50, and 1,000 knots). After every 25 knots is a bead, at which the Lord's Prayer can be recited, and at the end I say the Apostles' Creed. Prayer ropes can be purchased online (see the Resources section at the end of this book) and at many Orthodox churches.

THOUGHTS FOR YOUTH MINISTRY

While some of the contemplative practices, like Centering Prayer (see Chapter Six), are particularly difficult for youth, the Jesus Prayer can be accomplished. The recited prayer is concrete enough for the adolescent mind, and the addition of a prayer rope gives the practice a tangible quality that aids with success. That is, a student can set a goal of 100 or 200 recitations and achieve that fairly easily.

And, like Centering Prayer, the Jesus Prayer demands a mental discipline that is rarely required of adolescents. The constant focus—disciplining oneself not to think about schoolwork, conflict with parents, or a budding romance—is the exact opposite of the focus demanded by music videos, commercials, and video games.

As with many of the practices, it's best to teach the Prayer on a retreat where students succeed on the first attempts. The Prayer could be taught as part of a contemplative retreat and students could be given the opportunity to craft their own prayer ropes.

A FINAL WORD

Although I'll give the final word to Callistus and Ignatius, I do want to note first that the Jesus Prayer has become very significant to me, maybe more than any other practice I've investigated, and it's an important part of my Rule of Life. Now, here are Fathers Callistus and Ignatius:

When you will be worthy of the gift of ceaseless prayer in the heart, then, according to Isaac of Syria, you will have reached the summit of all virtues and become a dwelling place of the Holy Spirit; then the prayer will not cease, whether you sit, walk, eat, drink, or do anything else. Even in deep sleep prayer will be active in you without any effort, for even when it is externally silent, it continues secretly to act within. [Kadloubovsky and Palmer 270]

Chapter 06

Centering Prayer

Choose a suitable time for reflection and frequently consider the loving-kindness of God.

Thomas à Kempis

In 1989, the unthinkable happened to Dick and Carolyn: their 27-year-old son died in a car accident. It has been said that the most intense pain that a human being can experience is the death of a child. Dick and Carolyn wholeheartedly agree with this statement. They were plunged into deep darkness, not knowing where to turn for comfort. They felt as though they could not go on with life—they felt like lost souls, as though they had lost meaning in life.

As with most churches, theirs encouraged them to get into a support group, to talk it out in therapy, and to be faithful participants in worship. All these things helped, but the words all started to ring hollow—and it was a lot of words, between support groups, therapists, sermons, and wordy prayers. Still, deep within them both was an almost indescribable pain, a deep, piercing pain that kept them up at night and brought them to tears at inopportune moments.

And then, a while after their son's death, they read *Healing into Life and Death* by Stephen Levine. Prompted by this book, Dick and Carolyn decided to go on a retreat and try Centering Prayer. Although they had never heard of it before, these two grieving parents were open to just about anything that might assuage their pain. They went to the Villa Maria Retreat Center in southern Minnesota (the same place where I attended Sabbath!) and learned this ancient/modern art from the Ursuline nuns there.

"After three years of daily Centering Prayer the pain was gone," Dick told me. "I still miss my son, but the pain, loss, and grief that had paralyzed me for three years miraculously lifted. And the same thing happened for Carolyn."

Dick and Carolyn continue to practice Centering Prayer every day. It's the axis on which their spiritual lives pivot. And I think, if you met them, you would agree with me that they are two of the most joyous and peaceful Christians you've ever met.

HISTORY

Like the Jesus Prayer, Centering Prayer grew out of the reflections and writings of the Desert Fathers. John Cassian (c.360-c.430) came from the West and made a pilgrimage to the desert to learn the ways of contemplative prayer. After almost 20 years in the desert, Cassian was appointed a deacon in Constantinople, and by 415 he was in France where he established two monasteries, one for men and one for women. Cassian was deeply influenced by his time in the desert, and he wrote his book *The Conferences* about his conversations with the Desert Fathers to acquaint Western Christians with their teachings.

Cassian writes about one conference he had with Abba Isaac who taught him the essence of "true prayer." "To maintain an unceasing recollection of God, this formula must be ever before you," Abba Isaac told Cassian. "The formula is this: 'O God, come to my assistance; O Lord, make haste to help me.'" The result, Isaac said, is that "by God's light the mind mounts to the manifold knowledge of God, and thereafter feeds on mysteries loftier and more sacred…the prayer wherein, like a spark leaping up from a fire, the mind is rapt upward, and, destitute of the aid of senses or of anything visible or material, pours out its prayers to God." [Pennington (1980) 11,12]

Cassian's approach to contemplative prayer was the primary monastic practice for 10 centuries in the West, influencing Benedict, among others. During the Scholastic period (12th-15th centuries), theologians like Thomas Aquinas brought the West out of the Dark Ages by recovering the works of Aristotle and other ancient thinkers. As a result, intellectual theology became the "Queen of the Sciences," and spirituality was demoted to a remnant of the superstitious past.

In the 14th century, just as the form of the Jesus Prayer was becoming concrete in the East, a mystic in England who remained anonymous by choice, wrote the first spiritual classic in our language, *The Cloud of Unknowing*. Rebelling against the intellectual currents of the day, the author of *The Cloud* urges a return to "prayer of the heart." In 75 admonitions to his spiritual disciple, the author teaches a method of prayer in which the pray-er ascends above the "cloud of forgetting" where all creatures and all thoughts dwell, and rises toward the "cloud of unknowing" in which God dwells. Of course, these aren't physical locales, but existential realities, bringing the contemplative into the "mystical silence" between the two clouds.

The basic method promoted in *The Cloud* is to move beyond

thinking into a place of utter stillness with the Lord:

Here is what you are to do: lift your heart up to the Lord, with a gentle stirring of love desiring him for his own sake and not for his gifts. Center all your attention and desire on him and let this be the sole concern of your mind and heart. Do all in your power to forget everything else, keeping your thoughts and desires free from involvement with any of God's creatures or their affairs in general or in particular. Perhaps this will seem like an irresponsible attitude, but I tell you, let them all be; pay no attention to them. [Johnston ch. 3]

Unlike the Jesus Prayer, a repetitive prayer is not used. The prayer is encouraged to choose a simple, monosyllabic word, like "love" or "God." When the mind is distracted, this word is used to bring the mind back to focus on God: "Should some thought go on annoying you demanding to know what you are doing, answer with this one word alone." [Johnston ch. 7] This is true mental quiet, dwelling with God who came to Elijah in the "sheer silence." [1 Kings 19:12 NRSV] The result of practiced contemplation, promises the author, is an experience of the fullness of God's love.

The Cloud was widely read and much loved by English speakers of its day, but the intellectual emphasis of Scholasticism ultimately overwhelmed mystical and spiritual writings in influence. In the latter half of the 20th century, however, Christians were looking for sources of contemplation, meditation, and mysticism. As the world became more connected and "grew smaller," Eastern traditions infiltrated the West. In the 1960s and 1970s, Yoga (a Hindu practice), Zen Buddhism, Transcendental Meditation, and other forms of Eastern meditation influenced thousands of Americans. In response, some Trappist monks looked to Cassian and The Cloud as well as to St. Theresa of Ávila and St. John of the Cross for guidance. They distilled these teachings into a Christian method of contemplative prayer that has become known as Centering Prayer.

THEOLOGY

We have already noted the theological and spiritual influences of the East on John Cassian. Cassian opposed the radical grace of Augustine, the dominant theologian of his (or any) day. Whereas Augustine argued that humans are totally dependent on God's grace for salvation, Cassian held that humans take the first step toward God, choosing him, and then God's grace kicks in. This idea (known as Semipelagianism) is seen in Cassian's practice of prayer: the believer must first achieve a state of silence and contemplation, and then God works in the believer's heart. While Cassian's theology wouldn't be considered particularly unorthodox by many today, in his day it wasn't politically wise to oppose Augustine, and so Cassian's writings were originally influential only in France.

Another theological charge that has been leveled against *The Cloud* is Quietism. In the 17th century, some in France took the writings of St. Theresa of Ávila, who promoted a "prayer of quiet," to ridiculous extremes. Quietists taught the pray-er to become utterly passive, to the point of annihilating the will. Any thought, even of Christ or the cross or one's own salvation was rejected. This led to great moral laxity, since outward behaviors had no influence on the inner quiet of the person.

For good reason, Quietism was condemned in 1687 and died out shortly thereafter.

Centering Prayer, however, isn't quietistic. As opposed to annihilating the will, the pray-er moves into God's presence and rests there. The human will isn't destroyed; it finds peace in its true home. The contemplative person first acknowledges the love that God has for his creation and then quiets the mind to rest in, center on, and contemplate that love.

In fact, the author of *The Cloud* goes to great lengths to relate the Christ-centeredness of the Prayer. For several chapters he reflects on the story from Luke's Gospel in which Martha is busy preparing a meal for Jesus while Mary sits quietly at his feet. [Luke 10:38-42] While Martha goes about the necessary tasks of the "active life," Mary exemplifies the "contemplative life." Mary seems quite unconcerned with the activity around her, content to sit at Jesus' feet and rest in his presence. Of Martha's work, Mary "forgot all of this and was totally absorbed in the highest wisdom of God concealed in the obscurity of his humanity.... Mary turned to Jesus with all the love of her heart.... She sat there in perfect stillness with her heart's secret, joyous love intent upon that *cloud of unknowing* between her and her

God." [Johnston ch. 17]

The Cloud's author imagines that Mary isn't reflecting on Jesus' body or voice or odor, but has moved beyond images and senses to center on Jesus the Christ, her Christ. She is basking in his love for her. This makes Centering Prayer different from Ignatian meditation, for instance, where the pray-er places him or herself in the biblical narrative and attends to the sights and sounds and smells around.

M. Basil Pennington, one of the Trappist monks who has developed the modern practice of Centering Prayer, writes, "Centering Prayer is an opening, a response, a putting aside of all the debris that stands in the way of our being totally present to the present Lord, so that he can be present to us. It is a laying aside of thoughts, so that the heart can attend immediately to him." [Pennington(1980) 64, 65] This method neither replaces nor subjugates other forms of prayer, but in fact enhances them—prayers of praise, petition, intercession, and the like then spring from gratitude, from a deep experience of God's love.

PRACTICE

It might seem that the only instruction necessary for Centering Prayer is, "Be Quiet." But indeed a method to the practice is necessary. Basil Pennington describes the necessity thus:

The method of Centering Prayer is like a trellis. It is of the very nature of a climbing rose to reach up toward the sun and blossom forth. But without a trellis it keeps falling back on itself, and soon we have a large knotted mass that does not rise very high and gives birth to very few blooms. But if the climbing rose is given the support of a trellis, it can reach up and up toward the sun—the Sun of Justice and Life—and bear an ever greater abundance of blossoms. [Pennington(1980) 74]

The work of Pennington and other Trappist monks of St. Joseph's Abbey in Spencer, Massachusetts has been to compose this method. While the number of steps varies between authors, the basic formulation is this:

❶ As you sit comfortably with your eyes closed, let yourself settle down. Let go of all the thoughts, tensions, and sensations you may feel and begin to rest in the love of God who dwells within.

❷ Effortlessly, take up a word, the symbol of your intention to surrender to God's presence, and let the word be gently present. The word should be one syllable, if possible, and should communicate God's love to you.

❸ When you become aware of thoughts or as internal sensations arise, just take this as your signal to gently return to the word, the symbol of your intention to let go and rest in God's presence.

❹ If thoughts subside and you find yourself restfully aware, simply let go even of the word. Just be in that stillness. When thoughts begin to stir again, gently return to the word. Use the one word as your only response to thoughts, questions, or anxieties that arise in your mind.

❺ At the end of your prayer time (20 minutes in the morning and evening is a good balance), take a couple of minutes to come out of the silence—even if you don't feel you need it. Many people find this a perfect time to internally express to God their thanks and to pray for others in need of God's grace. The Lord's Prayer, slowly recited, is another gentle way to come out of the prayer. [adapted from www.lectiodivina.org/centering]

Centering Prayer takes time. In our noisy world it's extremely difficult to quiet down at all—in fact, it's even difficult to find a place that's quiet for 20 minutes. So, of course, Centering Prayer takes discipline: first the discipline to find the time and place for it, and then the mental discipline to not follow the rabbit trails that our active minds so often try to lead us down.

And the result of Centering Prayer is *not* a word from the Lord or any sort of divine revelation. Experts in the Prayer emphasize that the pray-er should have no goals in mind for the practice. In fact, the Prayer comes to fruition not in the minutes it is practiced, but throughout the day and throughout life. And, as it should be, that *fruition* is most often the fruit of the Spirit: love, joy, peace, patience, kindness, generosity, faithfulness, gentleness, and self-control. [Galatians 5:22-23]

This was tough. I've never tried centering prayer before, and I really didn't even know what it was. I guess I'd sum it up as being about 1) the present, and 2) God's love. We weren't given too much instruction, just to sit or stand or lie still for 45 minutes, to control our breathing, and to use a name or image for God repetitively. We were taken on a guided meditation in which we met up with Jesus on a road and sat with him on a bench to talk. It was very cool, and I really got stuck on the moment when Jesus and I met on the road—I suddenly became a little boy, maybe 8 years old, and I threw my arms around Jesus' waist and buried my head in his tummy. And I was hanging on to him for dear life—I don't think we ever made it to the bench to talk!

When it came time to center, I felt like I should focus on the phrase, Good Shepherd. Breathe in, "Good," breathe out, "Shepherd." The first 15 minutes were a bust—the woman next to me fell asleep and was snoring, and I was lying down. So I stood up and moved to another place in the room. It is sad to admit how much my mind wandered, especially to future things, just as they told us it would. I constantly found myself somewhere else, and I had to bring myself back to "Good Shepherd"—even though I never stopped repeating the phrase, I still wandered.

BUT, something very cool did happen—I got into it enough to lose track of time. I was disciplined enough not to look at the clock, not even to open my eyes at the beginning when I was tempted to. That temptation passed, and I must have gotten centered, because I wasn't expecting it or ready for it when the leader said, "Amen," at the end. That was cool!

THOUGHTS FOR YOUTH MINISTRY

To be honest, there may be no practice in this book more difficult for an adolescent than Centering Prayer. The stillness required not only runs counter to everything in adolescent culture, it's contrary to the physiology of adolescence. And yet, those of us who work with youth know that, even though their bodies are telling them to run, run, run, and the media is barraging them with thousands of images per day, our students *like* to slow down. In fact, they *need* to slow down.

I know a dad who, every morning before work, lights a candle for each of his children and sits in silence before God. When the children come down for breakfast, they see the burned candle and know that Dad has prayed for them and has been in God's presence. Now, as the children are getting older, they are occasionally joining Dad in his silent meditation. He doesn't really explain what he's doing, and they don't really need an explanation. My point is that even young children, when it's modeled for them, can be quiet in God's presence.

Basil Pennington agrees:

I should think that this kind of prayer could not only be attractive to young people but greatly help them in working through their identity struggles. Adolescents often like to go off by themselves to "get in touch" and just kind of "be with" things. To give them a little method to do this and to give them a sense of God's presence, that in some way Jesus is with them and they have in him a loving and caring friend, can be a priceless gift. [Pennington (1980) 145]

It can be taught at a retreat or in a small group, always by someone who's experienced in the method. The leader should keep track of the time so the students aren't tempted to keep checking a clock. Make sure all of the students have used the bathroom and are sitting comfortably. Don't do it right after a meal, and don't do it the morning after staying up until 2 a.m. (And don't do it at a lock-in!) The students should be alert, with empty stomachs and open minds. The leader must calmly describe Centering Prayer and gently lead the students into the exercise. I'd suggest that you don't just teach it once, during a smorgasbord retreat of spiritual practices, but have three or four times set aside for Centering Prayer so that students see how they get better at quieting the more they try it.

A FINAL WORD

From *The Cloud of Unknowing:*

There are some who believe that contemplation is so difficult and so terrible an experience that no one may reach it without great struggle and then only relish it rarely in those moments of ecstasy called ravishing. Let me answer these folk as best I can.

The truth is that God, in his wisdom, determines the course and the character of each one's contemplative journey according to the talents and gifts he has given. It is true that some people do not reach contemplation without long and arduous spiritual toil and even then only now and again know its perfection in the delight of ecstasy called ravishing. Yet, there are others so spiritually refined by grace and so intimate with God in prayer that they seem to possess and experience the perfection of this work almost as they like, even in the midst of their ordinary daily routine, whether sitting, standing, walking, or kneeling. They manage to retain full control and use of their physical and spiritual faculties at all times. [Johnston ch. 71]

There may be a true contemplative in your youth ministry, some student to whom Centering Prayer comes so easily that you feel like a novice in comparison…but you'll never know unless you open the door for your students to pray in this way.

Chapter 07

Meditation

If you avoid unnecessary talk and aimless visits, listening to news and gossip, you will find plenty of time to spend in meditation on holy things.

Thomas à Kempis

Damien O'Farrell is the youth pastor at Bridges Christian Fellowship in Riverside, California. He wrote this:

The summer between my junior and senior years in high school I attended a leadership retreat where I first experienced visualization and meditation. To this day, I vividly remember the voice of the instructor reminding us to breathe deeply and relax as he created a very basic outline for our visualized meditative journey. In that journey, the instructor led us up a mountain path to a quiet place where we conversed and poured out our soul to whomever our heart desired. (In my journey, I went to a cozy cabin, and talked to my grandfather who had died several years before.) The mental images I produced that day are forever burned into my memory, but even more than I remember those images, I remember how incredibly relaxed and centered I felt as I walked away from that experience. Those 20 minutes were worth at least four hours of sleep to my mind and spirit.

A few years later, in the midst of a hectic schedule and pressures from several areas of my life (ministry, family, school, work, etc.), I found myself reflecting on that sense of centeredness and rest and began longing for it once again. As a result of my workaholic tendencies, lack of sleep, and multitasking I had become emotionally, mentally, and spiritually exhausted, and the only place that I knew to turn for help was prayer and time with the Father, but it wasn't working. My prayers were, at best, self-centered, jumbled, and distracted, and they offered no peace or direction. Of course I knew in my mind that God was the same as he'd always been, and that he was listening, but I was far from hearing him. It was at that point that I began using visualization and meditation as a regular part of my prayer life, and it was at that point that I rediscovered that peace I was missing.

One day I suddenly realized that I didn't have as much trouble focusing when I was praising God through singing, when I was somewhere away from the distractions of everyday life, or when I could look at God's creation in nature. Obviously, I couldn't physically go to a place that met those criteria every time I needed or wanted prayer, but I realized that I could go there mentally. At first I questioned whether this technique was okay for a Christian to use. After all, I didn't want to just trick myself into an emotional feeling of peace, become dependent on those feelings, or head down a path away from orthodox Christianity. However, I soon reconciled myself to the fact that when I sing songs to God, I usually picture him or whatever I'm singing about, and those images help me connect with the words and focus my attention and praise on God. Therefore, creating the same types of pictures or focused experiences in my personal prayer time is no different, and is perfectly permissible. With that assurance, I began by using the visualization I used in my high school experience (walking up a mountain path), but this time I stopped at a rock with a view along the way, and had a focused and centering conversation with the Father once again. Eventually I began using other scenes (deserts, oceans, etc.) and started using the Bible as a guide for new visions of God, places of focused conversation with God (as opposed to the one-sided demands that we often call "prayer"), and experiences of God's character (e.g., love, grace, justice, etc.). The sixth chapter of the book of Isaiah is my all-time favorite guide!

Two years ago, it dawned on me that the pressures and frustrations that led me toward using visualization and meditation in my personal prayer times make up the daily life experience of teenagers. Not only that, but a just few conversations about prayer with teenagers convinced me that distraction, self-centeredness, and doubt infiltrate that area of their spiritual lives as well. So I began sharing my experience with the teenagers in my youth ministry, and began showing them how they could incorporate visualization and meditation into their own prayer times. We have used meditation and visualization in a number of different ways within our ministry:

→ We've started by reading a section of Scripture and encouraging the students to "close your eyes and let the Scripture sink in to your heads and hearts. Then imagine or visualize that piece of Scripture, and then watch and listen to what God wants to tell you." We have used this technique as an example of one way to focus and connect with God or a section of Scripture (like Isaiah 6) and listen during prayer time.

→ By guiding them through a visualization of journeying through a hot, dry, and barren desert, dragging a heavy load upon their shoulders, and then coming upon a man with cool water to drink and an easy load to carry in exchange for their own, we have taught and helped the students experience the nature of God. (Other similar visualizations might put them in a jungle where they fight their way to the place of rest, etc.)

→ By guiding them in a visualization to a quiet and empty place, instructing them to identify their hurts, distractions, and fears, and encouraging them to place those behind them, we have helped them quiet their hearts and understand the significance of a certain Scripture. It's also a way to help them focus their prayers on others, such as those who are lost and hurting, or confused and needing answers.

Honestly, the response that we've received from the seventh –12th graders within our ministry has surprised me. I expected a few of our deeper thinkers or artsy kids to dig it, and for the rest of the students to get lost or "weirded out." But the response has been overwhelmingly positive. We've found that meditation and visualization have created a space in which students make a personal and individual connection with the unseen (i.e., God and scriptural truths) and find answers on their own rather than at the instruction of an "all-knowing youth leader." Some of the truths that our students have discovered in their own personal prayer time have been far beyond any Sunday school lesson. God willing, these images and experiences will be forever burned in their memories and will continually help foster a true and impacting life journey with God.

Here are some e-mails from our students:

Daley: I personally like the visualizations…I think they're just cool cuz they help u think….I mean it's kinda hard to lose your train of thought when someone is speaking them (THOUGHTS) (that was capitalized for no general reason…I just hit the caps) to you. That's the part I really like about them cuz I always lose my train of thought and I start staring at the ceiling or the couch stuffing or something. I think it's also kind of a good way to start your message cuz it shuts everyone up and I think it really helps to start the brain tickin'…therefore possibly taking in more of what you are speaking about. :)

Michelle: After trying those visualizations it helped me find another way to worship God other than singing! If I can picture God and praise him as we walk together in a jungle, forest, or just sitting next to water, it makes it a whole new experience.

Lindsay: Thank you so much for doing the whole visualization thing. Many times before prayer I visually clear my head, thinking as you told us one time of the things on my mind and then push them aside. It's so amazing and has really helped me focus especially when I'm stressed.

HISTORY

In his opening words to Joshua after Moses' death, the Lord tells the new leader to meditate on his Word day and night. After that, the Psalmist urges us to meditate more than a dozen times. The word is absent from the New Testament, although the King James Version does translate 1 Timothy 4:15, "Meditate upon these things; give thyself wholly to them; that thy profiting may appear to all."

The modern conception of meditation, however, doesn't have a long history—that is, meditation as considered distinct from contemplative prayer. As a method of inner quieting, Judeo-Christian meditation goes back as far as Joshua and Psalm 46, "Be still and know…." As a Christian practice, it's inextricably bound up with the previous three chapters: silence, the Jesus Prayer, and Centering Prayer, as well as with the next chapter, the Ignatian Examen.

Further, it's linked with the recent popularity in the West of Eastern religions, resulting in books with such titles as *Christian Zen* and *Christian Yoga*. While this makes some Christians nervous, others revel in the fact that God is revealed in all truth, no matter the religion of origin. But before delving into these controversial waters, we must talk terminology and distinguish the two types of Christian meditation.

There is some debate within Christian circles about the terms *meditation* and *contemplation*. While Protestant Christians use the term *contemplation* fairly loosely, referring to quieter types of prayer, Catholics have a more strict definition of the word. To them, *contemplation* means true inner silence as has been achieved by only a few of the great saints of the church; whereas meditation has content, contemplation does not. While this book sticks with the Protestant understanding of the word, I acknowledge that most Catholics wouldn't use the word this way.

That being said, the more ancient type of meditation, and the more closely linked at times with Hinduism and Buddhism, is *apophatic* or *nondiscursive* meditation. In this method of meditation, the mind is emptied, much like Centering Prayer. No images or words are used in some forms of the practice, resulting in a total emptying, without even the "word" used in Centering Prayer. This type of meditation is an outgrowth of the Desert Fathers' writings, as well as John Cassian's *Ladder of Divine Ascent*, the writings of St. John of the Cross, and *The Cloud of Unknowing* mentioned previously.

At the end of the 20th century, Benedictine monk John Main

I led a college group today in a guided meditation. I had them imagine a walk with Jesus and finally sitting with the Lord on a bench and having a conversation with him. I was amazed, as I always am, at how effective this is at leading people into Jesus' presence. Many were in tears as they wrote down their conversations with him. Some ran back to their rooms to get their journals, one knelt with her arms upraised for more than an hour, another lay prostrate on the floor. Very moving.

What's somewhat incredible to me is how infrequently we do this—imagine ourselves sitting on a bench with Jesus, imagine hugging him, imagine him smiling at us. And how, when we do it, we're really reminded how much he loves us.

pioneered a Christian form of meditation that was influenced by his study with a Hindu master. He taught a form of meditation using the word *maranatha* (Aramaic for 'Come, Lord') as a mantra. Sitting cross-legged, the meditator chants (either aloud or silently) "ma-ra-na-tha" for 20 minutes twice per day. The teachings of Brother Main and others became so popular that the Vatican's Congregation for the Doctrine of the Faith issued a letter to all Catholic bishops in 1989 entitled "Some Aspects of Christian Meditation" to guide the bishops in their leadership of churches that were using meditation.

The other type of Christian meditation is known as *discursive* or guided meditation. This method uses words and images to usher the believer into God's presence. Ignatius of Loyola is the most influential purveyor of discursive meditation. In the *Spiritual Exercises*, Ignatius teaches his readers to use their five senses to enter into a biblical scene. Once there, the meditator listens to the conversations taking place, smells the food, touches Christ's robe, and tastes the wine. *Discursive* means 'conversational', and Ignatius concludes these types of exercises by having the meditator imagine a conversation with Christ in the midst of the biblical scene—for instance, on the road to Emmaus.

Discursive meditation hasn't been used much outside of the Ignatian Exercises until recently. Protestants, influenced by Martin Luther's doctrine of *sola scriptura* (meaning 'Scripture alone'), have shied away from methods that interject anything into the biblical narrative. However, guided meditation has been used more recently across confessional lines, even to help believers find healing from eating disorders, sexual sin, and addictions.

Apophatic meditation has been altogether more controversial. Because Buddhist and Hindu meditation extol a similar self-emptying, many Christians are uncomfortable with it. And indeed, many of the proponents of apophatic meditation have admittedly been influenced by Eastern religions. But whereas the goal of Buddhist meditation is to completely empty the self, the Christian purpose for this emptying is to be filled with the love of God:

Therefore, one has to interpret correctly the teaching of those masters who recommend "emptying" the spirit of all sensible representations and of every concept, while remaining lovingly attentive to God. In this way, the person praying creates an empty space which can then be filled by the richness of God. However, the emptiness which God requires is that of the renunciation of personal selfishness, not necessarily that of the renunciation of those created things which he has given us and among which he has placed us. There is no doubt that in prayer one should concentrate entirely on God and as far as possible exclude the things of this world which bind us to our selfishness. On this topic St. Augustine is an excellent teacher: if you want to find God, he says, abandon the exterior world and re-enter into yourself. However, he continues, do not remain in yourself, but go beyond yourself because you are not God; he is deeper and greater than you. [www.vatican.va]

It seems likely that as our world becomes "smaller," as students sit in class next to Hindus and Buddhists, and as more people become interested in yoga and transcendental meditation, Christian meditation will gain popularity, too. If recent history is any indication, more controversy may come before the church finds an acceptable practice of meditation.

THEOLOGY

"Christian meditation can be nothing but loving, reflective, obedient contemplation of him who is God's self-expression. He is the very explanation of God and his teaching to us." [Balthasar 13] With this statement, theologian Hans Urs von Balthasar reminds us that the focus of Christian meditation must be Jesus Christ.

The great articulator of the Christocentric faith was the Apostle Paul, who established the doctrine of the real presence of the risen Christ in the heart of the believer. Confession of the lips and belief in the heart was his standard for salvation; and meditation, when rightly practiced, is a focusing of the heart on Christ.

I say "when rightly practiced" because there are numerous examples of a distortion of Christian meditation in the history of the church. But the orthodoxy of Christian meditation can be tested, for, when rightly practiced, it always leads to the same result: "Contemplative Christian prayer always leads to love of neighbor, to action, and to the acceptance of trials, and precisely because of this it draws one close to God." [www.vatican.va] Love of God and love of neighbor is the inevitable result of true Christian meditation, whether discursive or apophatic.

PRACTICE

As well as being Christocentric, Christian meditation depends upon a theology of the Holy Spirit. As Balthasar reminds us, "The vistas of God's Word unfold to the meditating Christian solely through the gift of the Divine Spirit." [Balthasar 27] Indeed, the Christian meditator knows that any result of meditation, whether it be "divinization" (mystical union with Christ) or "the dark night of the soul," is a gift of the Holy Spirit. And here's another place where the Christian differs from his Hindu and Buddhist peers: whereas their meditation is thoroughly human, in origin and result, Christian meditation is ultimately guided by God.

Finally, it will do us good to look at two Latin words. In Latin, the word for contemplation is *theoria* and the word for conversion is *praxis*. While *theoria* is related to theory and ideas, praxis is related to practical ideas and practice. In the theology of meditation, these two are inseparable—there is no contemplation without a resulting conversion. That is, we don't contemplate merely as a sign of self-sacrifice to God. We meditate in order to be changed, to be converted from old habits and sins and vices. Meditation, though it's silent and still, challenges us in rigorous ways.

Apophatic meditation requires silence. Like the Jesus Prayer and Centering Prayer, the self-emptying required demands that the meditator finds a place of true quiet where distractions will be at a minimum. Of course, mental distractions will still come, but over time and practice, these too can be overcome.

Some, like John Main, recommend a mantra: "Maranatha" or "Come, Lord Jesus," or something of the sort. A seated posture is recommended, either in a chair with both feet firmly on the ground or cross-legged on the floor. The goal of apophatic meditation is inner quiet which leads to peace; as well as abiding in heaven and over the earth, God also dwells within the believer. To be utterly quiet and go within gives the believer a much better chance to touch God within, and peace, compassion, and an increased ability to love result.

Discursive meditation often takes place in a group. Relative quiet is best, but the absolute quiet of apophatic meditation isn't required. A leader guides the group through a set of images or through a biblical story, pausing to allow the participants to imagine the scene. At the end of the group exercise, participants are often given the opportunity to reflect on their experience, sometimes aloud with other group members, or in their journals, or even by painting or drawing the scene they imagined.

Individuals may also practice discursive meditation by slowly reading a biblical scene repeatedly and then following Ignatius's recommendations for interacting with the scene with all five senses. Again, it's beneficial to journal about the experience afterwards in order to further understand it or at least have a record of the meditation.

Some Christian therapists use meditation in their clinical work, and many loan or sell tapes and CDs to their clients to guide them in a daily meditation. Similar tapes and CDs are available on the Internet, some dealing with specific issues like weight loss and smoking.

THOUGHTS FOR YOUTH MINISTRY

I distinctly remember sitting under a tree at Big Sandy Bible Camp in Northern Minnesota. It was the summer before my sophomore year in high school, and I was about to embark on the adventure of being a camp counselor for the first time. Paul, our youth pastor, sat all of the counselors under this tree; he asked us to be comfortable but not lie down. After a couple minutes of silence, he started to speak very slowly and gently:

Imagine yourself walking down a road. It's the path of your life. Imagine what the path looks like—is it curvy? Or straight? Hilly? Flat? Is it wide or narrow, surrounded by trees or by fields? You look down—is the path rocky? Sandy? Is it dirt? Maybe it's paved. What does it feel like under your feet? And up ahead, what's in your path? Does it look clear or are there hurdles in your way?

Something is in your hands. You've been carrying it a long time—it's something you brought with you, in your spirit, up to camp. Look at it. What does it look like? What does it feel like in your hands? Is it hot? Cold? Warm? Is it smooth? Prickly? Sharp? Rough? Is it heavy or light?

Now look up ahead. A figure is moving toward you. You can't

quite make out who it is, but he seems to know you and his pace quickens as he recognizes you. Now you can see, it's Jesus! He's coming closer. What's the expression on his face as he walks toward you? How do you feel? He says a word of greeting to you—what does he say? How do you feel? Do you say anything back?

Now Jesus is standing in front of you. What does he say? Now he's holding his hands out—he wants you to put what's in your hands into his hands. How does it feel as the object leaves your hands? Do you say anything to Jesus?

Now you and Jesus start to walk together—he's holding the object of yours. As the two of you walk along, what do you talk about? Imagine the conversation…

Twenty years later I can still remember the experience of making that discursive meditation before the campers arrived at camp. The feeling of having Jesus take a burden I'd been carrying was an enormous comfort to me at age 15, and it still is today. And the students with whom I work are so much more image-driven even than I was, that guided image meditation is an even more powerful tool today.

Another way I've experienced this type of "Journey with Jesus" meditation is to end it by sitting on a bench with Jesus to have a conversation. Participants are given a piece of paper with a line down the middle. On one side of the paper, they write their own words to Jesus, and on the other side Jesus' words back to them. This, too, is a powerful tool, because those of us who have been practicing Christians for a while usually know exactly what Jesus has to say to us when we ask him questions—or what questions he has for us.

We can use a similar method to guide students through a biblical scene, much as Ignatius taught. Any story of Jesus teaching or performing a miracle works, as does much of Acts and many stories from the Old Testament.

A FINAL WORD

Hans Urs von Balthasar has some words of warning for those of us whose prayers are mainly made up of requests for God:

When in meditation a Christian finds the mystery of God's fullness in his inner divine self-giving, manifested in Jesus Christ, in his Eucharist, and his Church, the Christian too will not find it difficult to find this fullness again in the world so apparently empty of God. If the person does not pray meditatively but only commends personal intentions to God, this refinding will prove to be much more difficult. Perhaps he has succeeded in acquiring a certain Christian disposition in which he makes petitions for himself, his dear ones, and whatever else is important to him without, however, letting himself be sufficiently concerned about God's infinite designs. When Christ requires his disciples to ask in his name (John 14:13), this implies that they must also pray with his universal sentiments, which only a meditating faith can impart. [Balthasar 86]

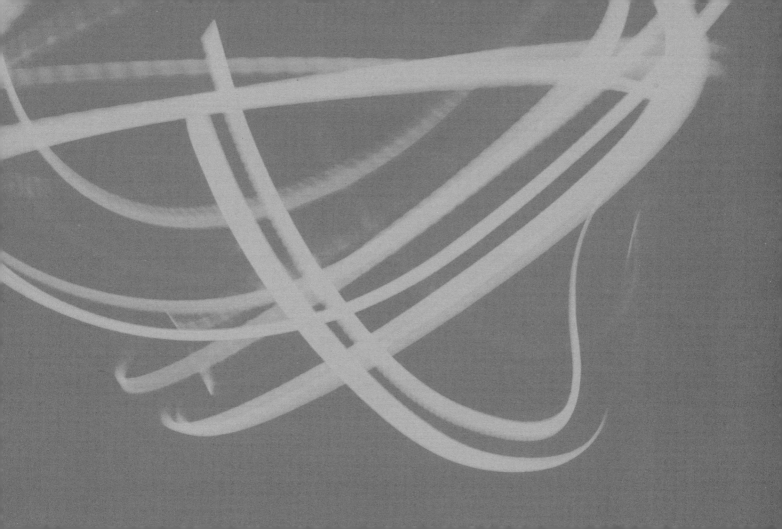

Chapter 08

The Ignatian Examen

Although we cannot always preserve our recollection, yet we must do so from time to time, and at least once a day, either in the morning or in the evening. In the morning form your intention, and at night examine your conduct, what you have done, said, and thought during the day, for in each of these you may have often offended both God and your neighbor.

Thomas à Kempis

Father Alan McGuckian is a Jesuit priest and the head of the Jesuit Communication Centre in Dublin, Ireland. In the late 1990s, he was overseeing a TV production studio and a radio program when his superiors asked him to design a Web site for the Jesuits of Ireland and England. He set about to do what most of us would—he planned to develop a site that would have information for men who were interested in joining the order, phone numbers, addresses, and bulletin boards for priests to share thoughts and ideas.

Being a novice to the Internet, Alan decided to spend some time surfing, getting acquainted with how the Internet works, finding which sites work better than others, and discovering what was most visually attractive. As Alan flipped through Web pages, the rhythm reminded him of something: it reminded him of "gated prayer" he had tried as a novitiate in India…and it reminded him of the rhythms of the Ignatian Prayer Examination, upon which Jesuit spiritual life is based.

Alan asked his fellow Jesuit, Peter Scally, if he might be able to design a Web site that takes people through a daily Ignatian Examen, and the result is *sacredspace.ie*, actually a hybrid of Ignatian prayer leading to a *lectio divina* on the lectionary-assigned Scripture passage for the day. *Sacredspace* is translated daily into 20 languages.

As I sat in his office in Dublin, Alan told me, "Before you go to prayer, consider how God looks at you." In other words, slow down, be quiet, even concentrate on your breath in order to calm yourself. On the *sacredspace* site, breathing is one of the first things mentioned, after the encouragement that this form of prayer can be done anywhere—at home, in a cathedral, or in a cubicle.

At the end of a *sacredspace* journey, you're taken to a Web page that shows how many people have visited *sacredspace* (at the time this book went to press, more than five and a half million since Lent, 1999). I commented to Alan on how overwhelming that number is, and he said, "There is power in the sense of community. *Sacredspace* helps people move from a lonely space into community—prayer always leads people to community."

I asked Alan, a man who has led millions of people in prayer through the Internet, if he had one word of advice for youth workers. He said this: "You can't guide other people to pray unless you pray yourself." Amen.

HISTORY

In the castle overlooking the city of Loyola, Spain, Ignatius was born in 1491. Born and reared in nobility, he spent his youth as many nobles do, traveling, learning the arts of literature and warfare, and sinning with abandon. He was devoted to the service of the Spanish king, serving both at court and in the army. In 1517, he joined the Spanish army, where the beginning of his life change happened in 1521. While he and his troops were defending the city of Pamplona, a French cannonball passed between his legs, heavily damaging his lower left leg. The French were kind enough to return him to Loyola where he underwent a long convalescence that included rebreaking and setting the leg, sawing off extra bone, and hanging weights from the leg to lengthen it to the size of his right leg.

During his recuperation, he asked for his favorite reading, tales of chivalric knights slaying foes and dragons and courting fair maidens. None of these was available, so he was instead given a history of the lives of the saints. As he read of the saints fasting and praying, preaching and healing, and of the many who gave their lives for the love of Christ, he noticed a difference in how it affected him: when he read the life of a knight, he ended up feeling dejected and sad, but when he read the life of a saint, he concluded with feelings of joy and peace.

Toward the end of his recovery, he saw a vision of the baby Jesus in Mary's arms, and he repented of all his past sins. Feeling that his forgiveness was complete, he began to speak only of spiritual things, and he vowed to serve Christ for the rest of his life.

He left Loyola for Montserrat where he spent three days in the sanctuary of the Benedictine monastery examining his life. Finally, he confessed his sins again, hung his sword on the altar, and put on the clothes of a beggar. In the days that followed, he lived in a nearby cave, praying and wondering if he had truly confessed *all* of his sins, even being tempted to commit suicide. Finally, with God's help he overcame these doubts and emerged from his solitude at peace and full of zeal for God's kingdom.

Ignatius then made a pilgrimage to the Holy Land, all the while taking notes on his spiritual experiences. He spent the next 11 years studying at various universities in Spain and France, often being persecuted for his radically spiritual life (two imprisonments, several beatings, and numerous expulsions from cities). By the end of his studies in Paris, nine men had joined him, and together they made vows of poverty and chastity in 1534. Three years later, this little brotherhood applied to Pope Paul III for official recognition by the Catholic Church, and the Society of Jesus, or Jesuits, was born. By the time of Ignatius's death in 1556, there were about 1,000 Jesuits—today there are more than 22,000.

Ignatius's *Book of Exercises* was written throughout most of his adult life—he was constantly reworking and revising it. It was published in 1541 and exists today in three early (though not original) editions, one in Spanish and two in Latin. It came at a time when the Roman Catholic Church was battling the early results of the Protestant Reformation, which added to its celebrity. It has been translated into hundreds of languages, and it constitutes the basis of the Jesuit life. Every Jesuit priest makes a 30-day retreat based on the *Exercises* at least twice during his training for the priesthood, and it serves as the basis of his annual retreat, too.

THEOLOGY

The *Spiritual Exercises* as they come to us today were the result of Ignatius's life work. He led many individuals through the Exercises on retreats throughout his lifetime, and he never stopped examining his own life: "the Exercises come from Ignatius' spiritual journey, characterized by following Jesus, practicing discernment, and acquiring a sense of service." [Wolff ix]

In Ignatius' own words, he developed "some spiritual exercises by which man is led to the possibility of conquering himself and deciding on a way of conducting his life that is free from harmful attachments." [Wolff 10] This happens by first examining one's own life in an incredibly thoroughgoing manner, and then meditating on the life, death, and resurrection of Christ. In so doing, individuals are led through confession and repentance to a place where they see Christ in the everyday things of life.

This happens most effectively, Ignatius writes, over the course of four weeks. The four weeks have been described like this:

1 *deformata reformare* (to reform what has been deformed by sin)

2 *reformata conformare* (to make what is thus reformed conform to the Divine model, Jesus)

PRACTICE

❸ *conformata confirmare* (to strengthen what thus conforms)

❹ *confirmata transformare* (to transform by love the already strengthened resolutions) [www.newadvent.org]

The author of Hebrews encourages a similar course of emulating the life of Christ as we shed the sins that bind us:

Therefore, since we are surrounded by such a great cloud of witnesses, let us throw off everything that hinders and the sin that so easily entangles, and let us run with perseverance the race marked out for us. Let us fix our eyes on Jesus, the author and perfecter of our faith, who for the joy set before him endured the cross, scorning its shame, and sat down at the right hand of the throne of God. [Hebrews 12:1-2]

Of course, self-examination has been a part of our story since close to the beginning. The Hebrews slaughtered a goat, or sent it out into the wilderness, after metaphorically laying their sins on it. Jesus was constantly challenging the Pharisees to examine not just their actions, but also their hearts. And Paul was notoriously tough on himself. In the Exercises, Ignatius developed a method of self-examination that has shaped hundreds of thousands of lives over the last half millennium.

The *Spiritual Exercises* are written from one retreat director to other retreat directors. Ignatius didn't write his Exercises for the individual believer, and it would be very difficult, if not impossible, to make the Exercises without a director. The Exercises is full of notations written to retreat directors on how to treat different individuals and issues that come up during a retreat. The retreat director becomes guide, confessor, and accountability partner, and so it requires a mature and spiritually sound person to fulfill that role.

The general model of examination is made on following five steps:

❶ To give thanks to God, our Lord, for all the benefits received

❷ To ask for his grace to know and expel our sins

❸ To question our soul about the sins committed during the same day, examining ourselves hour after hour from the time of our awakening, in thoughts, words, and actions, in the order given in the Particular Examination

❹ To ask forgiveness for the faults committed

❺ To propose with God's help to correct ourselves; then, afterward, to recite the Our Father. [Wolff 17]

Although Ignatius repeatedly encourages modification of the retreat depending on the advancement of the individual retreatant, the Exercises are based on a four-week model. Basically, on each day of the week, the retreatant spends five hour-long sessions in examination: midnight, dawn, morning, late afternoon, and evening. [Exercises an. 72] During each session, an intricate schedule of prayer, meditation, and colloquy (conversation with God) is followed.

During the first week, the retreatant meditates on sins committed, both in action and thought, and imagines confessing these sins to Jesus as he hangs on the cross. During the fifth exercise of the day, hell is imagined by all five senses as the consequence of the sins committed. Ignatius recommends that during the first week, "I avoid all thoughts that bring me joy…I deprive myself of the brightness of light…I absolutely refrain from laughing…I do not fix my eyes on anyone…[and] I add some kind of reparation or penance…wearing hair shirts, ropes, or chains." He also says the retreatant should have only moderate amounts of sleep and food. [Exercises an. 78-86]

The second week is a contemplation of the life of Jesus Christ, comparing him to an earthly king who is calling his subjects to war. From the first day, meditating on the incarnation and nativity of Jesus, through the final meditation of the week on Palm Sunday, the retreatant imagines Lucifer arrayed with all of his forces in one plain, ready to do battle, and Jesus and his forces lined up against him. By the end of this week, Ignatius says the retreatant will be ready to make Election—that is, to choose which army she wants to be a part of, to choose what kind of a person she wants to be.

The Passion of Christ is the focus of the third week. One imagines being at the Last Supper and in the Garden of Gethsemene, at the foot of the cross, and laying Jesus' body in the tomb. Ignatius tells us to imagine the conversation at the Last Supper, how the disciples ate and what they ate, and how it felt to have your feet washed by the Lord. He also suggests abstinence from all food and drink except bread and water during the third week.

Central to the fourth week is the contemplation on Christ's postresurrection appearances and the joy and victory they signify. It culminates in the contemplation for achieving Divine Love. In this series of contemplations, Ignatius points the retreatant toward a mystical appreciation of the Divine Love that permeates and holds all reality in being. As a response to all God's activity, in creation and redemption, the following prayer of complete self-surrender is proposed:

Take, Lord, all my freedom. Accept all my memory, intellect, and will. All that I have or possess, you have given to me; all I give back to you, and give up then to be governed by your will. Grant me only the grace to love you, and I am sufficiently rich so that I do not ask for anything else. [Exercises an. 234]

The *Spiritual Exercises* concludes with dozens of notes on praying and on the Christian life.

THOUGHTS FOR YOUTH MINISTRY

First of all, to make the Exercises at some point in life should be a goal of every Christian. For those of us who aren't single, it can be difficult to think of extracting ourselves from ministry and family for 30 days, but it is, of course, a matter of enormous commitment. Around the world, retreat centers and monasteries are always leading Ignatian retreats, some 30 days, but many shorter, too.

Having been on one or more Ignatian retreats, it would be very possible to adapt the principles of Ignatius for use on a youth retreat, or (think of it!) a 30-day Ignatian summer camp. In fact, some retreats around the country already incorporate Ignatian methods and patterns e.g., T.E.C. (Teens Encounter Christ), L.O.G. (Love of God), and Kairos.

At Georgetown Prep School in North Bethesda, Maryland, the senior boys are given the chance to spend a semester working through the Exercises according to the Nineteenth Annotation, which gives a method of more application of the Exercises. Each young man is assigned a guide who is familiar with the Exercises. The adult guides the student through the Exercises with four 20-minute prayer sessions per week. Some make it through the first section of Ignatius's four "weeks," and others make it through more.

As a follow-up to its fall retreat for seniors, the staff at Georgetown Prep has found the Nineteenth Annotation enormously helpful in combating the postretreat letdown. When the seniors get back to school, still on the "mountain top," those who are interested are interviewed to see if they are mature enough for the rigors of the Exercises. The results are life changing: "You taught me how to talk to God," one student wrote as he headed off to college. "If I forget all the useless facts I learned…it will be fine because I will never forget what you showed me." [Collins 12]

More immediately, we might access the three methods of prayer that Ignatius outlines after week four. The first is a slow prayer in which an individual examines his life according to the Ten Commandments, the seven deadly sins, the three faculties of the soul, and the five senses. To begin, one contemplates the first commandment, confessing every time he has broken it. Upon running out of sins to confess, say the Lord's Prayer, and move on to the second commandment.

The second method of praying is to take a familiar prayer like the Lord's Prayer, and spend one hour meditating on a word or two ("Our Father"). At the end of the hour, one quickly says the rest of the prayer. The next day, the meditation is on the next word or two ("who art"), etc. The third method of praying combines the first two using the breath as the guide for meditation.

Another application to youth ministry is to rethink the way we normally do things. Often, when small groups meet, before getting to the lesson, group members go around the circle and tell about their "highs and lows" of the last week. Ignatius' version of this practice is to see life in terms of "consolations" and "desolations," (also translated "enlivening" and "stifling" of God's Spirit). A consolation is "when the soul takes fire in the love of its Creator by some inner motion…any increase of faith, hope, and charity can also be called consolation; equally all joyfulness, which usually incites the soul to meditation on heavenly things, to zeal for salvation, to be at rest and peace with God." [Exercises an. 316]

"On the contrary," Ignatius writes, "any obscuring of the soul, any disturbance, any instigation to inferior or earthly things, must be called spiritual desolation." Moments in which we feel far from God, doubt the Spirit's work in our lives, doubt our salvation, or doubt even the existence of God are desolations.

A FINAL WORD

[Exercises an. 317]

So, instead of measuring the week according to the fairly superficial "highs and lows" of what made them feel good and what didn't, students can examine the past week according to when the Spirit was moving or flowing in their lives versus when the Spirit was blocked or seemed far away. While many of the instances cited by students may be the same as what they would say for "highs and lows," "consolations and desolations" reorients the focus to be on God instead of on self. And this practice can sacralize the otherwise mundane moments in life.

A prayer from the *Spiritual Exercises*:

Here I am, O supreme King and Lord of all things, I, so unworthy, but still confiding on your grace and help, I offer myself entirely to you and submit all that is mine to your will. In the presence of your infinite Goodness, and under the sight of your glorious Virgin Mother and of the whole heavenly court, I declare that this is my intention, my desire, and my firm decision: Provided it will be for your greatest praise and for my best obedience to you, to follow you as nearly as possible and to imitate you in bearing injustices and adversities, with true poverty, of spirit and things as well, if it pleases your holiest Majesty to elect and accept me for such a stage of life. [Exercises an. 98]

Chapter 09
Icons

We must revere Christ above all things, and live purely in his sight as angels.

Thomas à Kempis

Father Nicholas Speier is the pastor of St. Athanasius Orthodox Church in Goleta, California. He writes:

As a youth worker I've given many talks on confession and on the need to repent of our sins so they don't fester as unkept sores or root in us as bad habits. In speaking with the teens, it is important to use the right words, but more, those talks need to be in the right place.

Bringing the youth to the church with the holy images around them is a tremendous aid in helping them to see their sins and bringing them to a deep repentance. Two experiences come to mind.

Years ago at the beginning of a Lenten season we had our youth at the church for a prayer service, a time of quiet, and to give them the opportunity for self-examination. The teens were thorough in their confessions and were influenced by the holiness depicted around them in the icons of the Lord, the holy virgin, and all the saints gone before them. I remember this as a profound experience with them in getting deeply into their souls. The soberness they felt standing before the icon of Christ, the example of purity we see in the Virgin Mary, or call to repentance from St. John the Baptist led them to profound confession. This would have been much more difficult and less productive in a living room or teen room without the aid of the icons.

A second experience was at a camp retreat with our teens. The camp setting is wonderful and is always a great time. When it comes time to talk about repentance and for their times of confession, it becomes essential to go into the chapel. The youth immediately begin to sense the presence of Christ and the saints and it moves them to repentance. More than once have I seen teens be given insight into their struggles, and relief from the same. It takes a great deal of courage to confess the deep-rooted, embarrassing sins, but all around them stand examples of confessing saints, purity of life, and the power of forgiveness.

A monk of the Eastern church says:

Contact with absolute holiness cannot but cause a sinner moral agony, for, as with the woman taken in adultery, the silent presence of this holiness is, in itself, a judgment and condemnation. If very few Christians have a lively and agonizing awareness of their sins, it is because Jesus is not truly present to them. We touch here on a point which is important, and that concerns

HISTORY

'evangelization' and 'conversion': one does not progress from the consciousness of sin to the presence of Jesus, but, on the contrary, it is from the presence of Jesus that one becomes conscious of sin. It is the way we look at Jesus (or, rather, our awareness of the way that Jesus looks at us) which produces repentance in us. [The Year of Grace of our Lord 17]

These words very much mirror my experience with youth struggling with sin but desiring to move forward in their faith. Being in the presence of holy icons helps them see "the way Jesus looks at them"—with compassion and a desire to forgive.

According to legend, the first icon (*icon* is Greek for 'image') was made by Jesus himself. In an extrabiblical story kept alive by the church, King Abgar of Edessa was dying of leprosy in North Africa and sent an emissary, Ananias, to ask Jesus to come to Edessa and heal him. Ananias was instructed to paint a picture of Jesus if a visit to Edessa was not possible. Jesus declined traveling to Edessa, for he was only days away from his Passion, but when he saw Ananias trying to paint his picture through the heavy crowds, Jesus took pity on him. After washing his face, Jesus dried his face with a square of linen, leaving a near-perfect imprint of his image on the cloth.

Ananias took the linen back to Edessa and King Abgar was healed immediately upon seeing it. After Pentecost, Thaddeus (a.k.a. St. Jude) took a missionary journey to Edessa, and Edessa became the first officially Christian nation in the late second century. The *acheiropoietos* (ak-air-o-póy-a-tos), the 'icon made without human hands', stayed in Edessa until 951, when it was sent to Constantinople to heal the ailing Emperor Romanus. In 1204, Constantinople was sacked by the Crusaders and the famous icon was taken to Italy. Its whereabouts today are unknown.

This morning the Hippses and I went to St. Anthony's Greek Orthodox Church in Pasadena. Having used the Divine Liturgy of St. Chrysostom, I was quite familiar with the order of the service. Also, my knowledge of Greek was indispensable, for about half of the service was in Greek.

I think that the Divine Liturgy is one of the most beautiful things ever written—it seems that every word is carefully chosen, no throwaway lines. It was sung, except where the congregation joined in for the Lord's Prayer and the Nicene Creed. Both the priest and the choir delivered the liturgy wonderfully.

...So, it was a wonder to me that at 10 a.m., when the liturgy began, there were only five people in the sanctuary, including us. By 11 a.m., when the "preliminaries" were over and the procession to the communion began, the place was nearly full.

What was best of all, I think, was the sun coming through the windows and illuminating the dozens of icons on the iconostasis. I don't know much about icons (yet), but there is something mesmerizing and otherworldly about them. I know that as an evangelical I'm supposed to be suspicious of icons, but there is something strangely compelling about them. I definitely want to learn more.

In similar stories, St. Luke, a physician and, according to legend, a painter, painted five portraits of Mary while she was still alive. One of these, an icon of Mary with the baby Jesus, was given to her as a gift. And, as we observe in the Stations of the Cross, another tradition has Veronica (*vera icona*, 'true image') handing Jesus a cloth to wipe his face as he carried his Cross to Golgotha—this icon is kept in one of the massive piers that supports the cupola of St. Peter's basilica in Rome. The Shroud of Turin (supposedly the linen in which Jesus was wrapped in the tomb), the authenticity of which is often debated, is another such legendary object.

All of these stories tie the origin of iconography to Jesus himself. And, indeed, there is much to suggest that, even if these stories are all fictional, portraits of Jesus were painted while those who knew him were still alive. Second-century Christians painted many images, though none of Jesus, in the catacombs of Rome and throughout the Empire. Mosaic and carved wooden representations of Jesus survive in Rome from the fourth century, and St. Catherine's monastery at the base of Mt. Sinai has traditional icons of Jesus and Peter dating from the sixth century. Jim Forest notes that iconographers often spruced up images that had gotten dark and dirty over the years with brighter paint; he piques our imaginations with this suggestion: "Perhaps at the foundation level of one or another ancient icon are brush strokes that were made by the hand of St. Luke." [Forest 4]

Icons have always held an important place in the imagination and faith of Eastern Christians. While some of the early church fathers condemned the use of icons, the people, never altogether impressed with theological battles, made icons a central aspect of their practice of Christianity. The painting and reproduction of icons became more formalized in the second half of the first millennium, and their use was known across the Eastern world.

Icons also came under attack during this time. From the beginnings of the paintings, some theologians questioned whether praying to icons actually constituted idolatry, forbidden by the Second Commandment. In the first half of the eighth century, Emperor Leo III in Constantinople believed that the use of icons had gotten out of control, and he thought that their use was an obstacle to the evangelism of Jews and Muslims. In 726 he issued an edict ordering the destruction of all icons. Although his actions were condemned by the pope and persuasively put down in a theological treatise by John of Damascus, the "Iconoclastic Controversy" continued until 784. During that time, thousands of icons were destroyed, many iconographers had their hands chopped off, and many monks fled to the West with icons hidden under their robes.

Empress Irene, who loved icons, convened the Seventh General Council of the church in Nicaea in 787. The council undid Leo's edict, set parameters on the veneration and painting of icons, and decreed the restoration of icons throughout the empire. The "Second Iconoclastic Controversy" broke out under Leo V and lasted another 28 years. Only in 843 were icons finally restored, and on the first Sunday of Lent that year, a great feast was held to celebrate the end of the controversy. To this day, the Eastern church celebrates the first Sunday of Lent as the "Feast of the Triumph of Orthodoxy."

In the East, the Iconoclastic Controversy among the educated clergy actually caused an increase in the use of icons among the masses. But in the West, there was great confusion about the theology behind the use of icons, mostly attributed to a mistranslation of the Acts of the Nicene Council. Sadly, this confusion combined with other theological and political friction that led to the Great Schism between East and West in 1054. To this day, icons are very significant in the theology of the Eastern Church but are virtually unknown in the West.

THEOLOGY

Most of the theological controversies and heresies of the early church (and many today) centered on the nature of Christ: Was he truly human? Was he truly divine? Was he more divine than he was human, or more human than he was divine? All sorts of cults and sects sprang up in the first five centuries of Christianity, each claiming to have the truth about Christ's true nature. And all of the top theologians rose to the challenge of rearticulating what Paul had made clear in his epistles: through some miraculous paradox, Jesus of Nazareth was fully human and fully divine.

When defending the painting and use of icons, St. John of Damascus and others argued for this very idea. If the second person of the Trinity, the Logos, became Jesus of Nazareth, and if Jesus of Nazareth was a real human being, then he could, and indeed should, be represented in paintings. In his treatise defending iconography, John of Damascus writes,

If we made an image of the invisible God, we would certainly be in error...but we do not do anything of the kind; we do not err, in fact, if we make the image of God incarnate who appeared on the earth in the flesh, who in his ineffable goodness, lived with men and assumed the nature, the volume, the form, and the color of the flesh. [Forest 8]

Simon Jenkins, a modern writer, agrees:

The point about icons is that they affirm the teaching, to quote the language of the Creed, that Jesus Christ is "the only-begotten Son of God" who "was made man." Simply to paint an image of Christ is to confess that Jesus, the Son of God, truly appeared on earth as a human being—"sprung from Mary as well as from God," in the words of St. Ignatius. It is to confess that "the Word made flesh" could be seen with the eyes. And conversely, to oppose the making of icons is to deny that confession.... [I]cons stand on the front line of the faith: they stand or fall on the truth of Christianity itself. [Jenkins 8-9]

But even if the painting of a portrait of Jesus can be justified theologically, what of the real danger that, when that portrait is an icon, it actually becomes an idol? To answer this question, we have to investigate an intricacy of Orthodox theology: the difference between *adoration* and *veneration*. Adoration is that form of human submission and worship that is due only to Almighty God. Adoration is what a creature gives the Creator. Adoration is worship.

Veneration, on the other hand, is how one uses an icon in prayer—not unlike the Bible, which we venerate and respect, but don't worship. The Bible brings us closer to God, guides us in prayer, and is considered a gift from God, even though it was written and translated by human hands. Similarly, an icon, painted by human hands, leads us into God's presence. In fact, the Nicene Council of 787 stated that it's not the icon that is venerated, but the ideal and perfect prototype on which the icon is based. Similarly, we might say we don't venerate the NIV or *The Message* translations but the original Greek and Hebrew manuscripts of the Bible, which are lost, but upon which our modern translations are based. Of course, Jesus himself is ultimately the prototype of all Christ icons.

Another example of this difference is the Catholic belief that Christians can pray *through* saints, especially the Blessed Virgin Mary, and their prayers will be delivered to the throne of God. I'll admit that, to a Protestant like me, the difference between praying through an icon or a saint is a nuance that I have a hard time grasping. However, I can understand the theological difference, and I respect the traditions under which they have developed. The bottom line is that we use icons to pray, but we do not pray to them—we pray *through* them.

Father Speier explained it to me like this: I ask friends to pray for me; in fact, I even ask friends on the phone, whom I cannot see, to pray for me. Since we believe that those who have died in faith are currently living in eternity with God, praying through an icon of a saint is simply asking one of these friends to pray for me.

PRACTICE

Seen in this way, it can be fun to think of ways to incorporate praying with icons into your personal devotional life and into your ministry. The first item of business is to get an icon. They are sold at many Orthodox churches and monasteries and they can also be ordered on the Internet. True icons are made in accordance with a very specific set of rules. Most often they are painted on a wooden panel using egg yolk-based tempera paint. A piece of linen is stretched over the wood, which acts as a canvas. Linseed oil is applied after the paint has dried to protect the image.

A limited number of poses is available to the iconographer. They all stem from the ancient icons—for instance, the portrait of Jesus' face alone is a replica of "The Icon Made without Human Hands"; and the "Icon of Loving-kindness" that shows the baby Jesus' face pressed against his mother's was supposedly first painted by Luke. Human models are never used to paint icons; only other icons are acceptable as models.

Shadows are never seen in a icon, and no source of light beams on the subject's face. The icon itself is a source of light: "The saintliness or the holiness of the person shines out from the entire body. The light of God saturates all things, therefore, the images on icons do not cast shadows." [Hallick 29] The parts of the anatomy associated with the five senses are exaggerated in size, since they're the windows to the soul, and the person in the icon looks straight ahead at the pray-er. Backgrounds are used only to identify the saint, so most icons of Jesus and/or Mary have no scenery.

Both the figures and the minimal scenery in an icon seem strange, even awkward, to modern, Western eyes. However an icon is not meant to be a depiction of a normal human being but of Jesus or Mary or a saint in their resurrected state—what Paul calls a "spiritual body" [1 Corinthians 15:44] and theologians call a "resurrection body." Reality is not what the artist is seeking. Neither is the icon meant to draw the viewer into a scene. Instead, the focal point of the icon is actually in front of the painting, where the viewer is standing, so an icon can be thought of as embracing the pray-er. Henri Nouwen's thoughts on this:

Icons are not easy to "see." They do not immediately speak to our senses. They do not excite, fascinate, stir our emotions, or stimulate our imagination. At first, they even seem somewhat rigid, lifeless, schematic, and dull. They do not reveal themselves to us at first sight. It is only gradually, after patient, prayerful presence that they start speaking to us. And as they speak, they speak more to our inner than to our outer senses. They speak to the heart that searches for God. [Nouwen (1987) 14]

Iconographers fast and pray while they are painting, making the creation of an icon a spiritual experience itself. Finally, if the image meets all the criteria, it's blessed by a priest and is ready for display in a church or home.

In an Orthodox church, icons are displayed on an *iconostasis*, a large screen that runs the width of the sanctuary and separates the sanctuary (where worshipers sit) from the nave (where the altar resides). As with most other aspects of Orthodox ecclesiology, the iconostasis gives a church an otherworldly and mysterious feel.

Most devout Orthodox families and individuals will have an "icon corner" in their home, always on an eastern wall so they will be facing Jerusalem if Jesus returns while they are at prayer. Actually, this practice is becoming more popular with all types of Christians—devoting some area of the home as "sacred space" with a candle, an icon or two, and a prayer book.

THOUGHTS FOR YOUTH MINISTRY

One would be hard-pressed to argue against the fact that the students with whom we work are the most image-driven generation of all time. While Christianity is a faith based on the written word of Scripture, we must take seriously our students' image-based lives. One way to do this is to incorporate icons into our ministries, for "…we do not have to be passive victims of a world that wants to entertain and distract us. We can make some decisions and choices. A spiritual life in the midst of our energy-draining society requires us to take conscious steps to safeguard that inner space where we can keep our eyes fixed on the beauty of the Lord." [Nouwen (1987) 12]

We have had an "icon night" at which students were briefly taught some of the basics of praying with icons, and then given the chance for extended periods of icon-based praying. We've acquired some real-life icons and we have other copies. But, no surprise, the icons we projected onto the big screen most captured the students' attention.

At some point in the night, students are challenged to think about what "icons" guide their lives, and how those symbols tempt them to idolatry—we've incorporated some video at this point, showing the usual suspects: the Nike swoosh, the

A FINAL WORD

Playboy bunny, the Hurley "H." We also allow them to draw and paint their own icons, making sure that they know what a serious and holy task a true iconographer has.

After a night like this, it's natural to erect an "icon corner" in the youth room, and to use icons prayerfully between songs during worship. It's also very appropriate to invite an Orthodox priest to come and teach about icons, or to go to a nearby Orthodox church for worship.

As with any spiritual practice, if the use of icons is outside of your tradition, it's advisable to enter cautiously and respectfully into another's tradition—cautiously because others in your church may not understand or agree, and respectfully so as not to offend those Christians for whom icon-based prayer is central to faith.

St. John of Damascus says in his defense of icons:

Previously there was absolutely no way in which God, who has neither a body nor a face, could be represented by any image. But now that he has made himself visible in the flesh and has lived with people, I can make an image of what I have seen of God…and contemplate the glory of the Lord, his face having been unveiled. [McGrath 61]

And a bonus from Henri Nouwen:

Icons…have imprinted themselves so deeply on my inner life that they appear every time I need comfort and consolation. There are many times when I cannot pray, when I am too tired to read the gospels, too restless to have spiritual thoughts, too depressed to find words for God, or too exhausted to do anything. But I can still look at these images so intimately connected with the experience of love. [Nouwen (1987) 11-12]

Chapter 10

Spiritual Direction

Do not flatter the wealthy, and avoid the society of the great. Associate rather with the humble and simple, the devout, and the virtuous, and converse with them on such things as edify.

Thomas à Kempis

Joan Stevenson is a youth pastor who has been in a fruitful relationship with a spiritual director for more than a year. She writes:

I was at yet another large youth minister's convention when all the hurry, loud music, and speakers just got to me. I felt empty and drained. I had been working 55 hours a week as a youth minister and still felt like I could barely get my head above water to catch a breath before being shoved underneath again by another event, another phone call, another crisis. While I was at this convention I heard of the Sabbath Retreat. I was intrigued. A youth minister's retreat all about rest? I signed up to go, not knowing what to expect.

At the Sabbath Retreat I was assigned to a spiritual direction group. Unlike a typical small group, in this group one person would share while everyone else prayerfully listened to what was said. No one interjected their thoughts or said, "Oh yeah, the same thing has happened to me." It was so refreshing to be listened to and to not worry about what others would say—to not be given advice. And as I shared I found that I was beginning to hear the voice of God.

My experience at the Sabbath Retreat changed me. I was given a taste of a different way of doing life—a way of doing life which involved rest, listening to God, and paying attention to what my body was telling me. I was so used to going through life exhausted. I came home from the retreat knowing I needed to find a spiritual director so that I could have some presence in my life reminding me that there was a different way of life and ministry. I was unsuccessful, and within a few months I was back in my same routine. But this time it was worse because I had a vision and a taste of how life could be.

A little more than a year later, I was faced with an unexplained medical problem that hit me on the first night of summer camp. I had to come home from camp, leaving my other leaders in charge. I felt so guilty. I didn't understand what was going on with me. I talked with my doctor, and he talked to me about making some lifestyle changes. I began to think again about what I learned on the Sabbath Retreat. I made some changes to my work schedule and family life. I cut back my ministry calendar. I took a weekly Sabbath day of rest and it took months before the exhaustion started to lift. In the process I connected with a spiritual director and began attending to the voice of God in my life.

I returned to the Sabbath Retreat two years after my first one.

HISTORY

What seemed like a nice but unattainable vision two years previous was becoming a reality in my life. Spiritual direction has contributed to this mostly by helping me to pay attention to what God is saying to me.

We all might long for the spiritual direction that Adam received when he walked with God in the garden "at the time of the evening breeze." We can only imagine that kind of direct guidance from the Lord. But that kind of direction isn't available to us. Fortunately, the Bible is rife with examples of spiritual companionship, both good and bad. From the spiritual friendship between David and Jonathan to the highly suspect advice of Job's "theologian" friends, Scripture gives some parameters for healthy spiritual direction.

One paradigmatic example takes place in 1 Samuel 3, when Samuel is confused by the voice he hears in the night. Eli, Samuel's spiritual father, "realized that the Lord was calling the boy." [1 Samuel 3:8] The Lord was moving in Samuel's life, speaking to him, in fact, but it took another who was older and more experienced in the movements of God to open Samuel's eyes and ears to God.

And, of course, the paramount model for spiritual direction is Jesus himself. A model of friendship, Jesus spent time with his disciples both individually and in groups. He asked questions, told stories, and guided his friends, sometimes gently and sometimes forcefully, toward the truth. In all things, he showed charity, love, and a deep desire for these men and women to grow spiritually. His guidance was not self-serving. He listened, both to things spoken and unspoken (think of the Samaritan woman at the well [John 4:7-30]). He read between the lines and got to the heart of the matter. He pointed to the movements of the Holy Spirit. He was called "Good Teacher." [Mark 10:17; Luke 18:18]

The Desert Fathers and Mothers got their titles, *Abba* and *Amma*, from offering this kind of guidance. As the reputation of the mystics on Mt. Athos and in the Egyptian and Syrian deserts grew, hundreds, and even thousands, of lay people and clerics made pilgrimages to see them. The Desert Fathers and Mothers considered it part of their vocation to lead their visitors into deeper holiness, to teach them the ways of contemplative prayer, and even to look into their lives with the charism of divine discernment. "You must prostrate yourselves before brothers who come to visit you," Abba Apollo said, "for it is not them but God you venerate." [Russell 78]

Their teaching might seem off-putting to us. Abba Isaac went to two different elder Fathers, hoping for spiritual guidance, but they only served him. Out of frustration, he asked what he must do to receive some spiritual direction, and the elder Abba answered him (in the third person), "As far as I am concerned, I do not tell him anything, but if he wishes he can do what he sees me doing." And so Isaac learned to work in silence as he saw his Father working in silence. [Guenther 52] In any case, it was expected that every Abba or Amma was under the tutelage of another Abba or Amma.

In the 12th century, Aelred of Rievaulx (1109-1166) wrote *Spiritual Friendship*. In it he commends a prototype for companions in spirit:

What happiness, what security, what joy to have someone to whom you dare to speak on terms of equality as to another self; one to whom you can unblushingly make known what progress you have made in the spiritual life; one to whom you can entrust all the secrets of your heart and before whom you can place all your plans. [Guenther 12]

In both Eastern Orthodox and Roman Catholic traditions, spiritual direction has been common among laity and mandatory among clergy. Recently, Protestants have become very interested in the practice, flocking to Catholic seminaries to earn certificates in spiritual direction. More Protestant seminaries are

THEOLOGY

offering similar certificates, evangelical publishers are producing books on the subject, and Youth Specialties now employs a spiritual director (SD) to help youth workers find a director.

Clearly, over the years, spiritual direction has taken on a more formal shape than when a believer sat at the feet of Jesus or of an Abba or Amma. Schools and seminaries train SDs, some retreat centers are staffed with SDs, and dozens of books in the last 20 years describe the process of direction. But at its heart, spiritual direction attempts to recreate that same environment in which Adam walked with God: a time of peace and listening to discover where God is moving in one's life.

God was Adam's companion. Joshua looked to Moses. Ruth placed herself under Naomi's direction. Elisha learned from Elijah. The 12 disciples followed Jesus. Timothy was Paul's companion. Peter walked the streets of Jerusalem with John. There is no dearth of examples in Scripture for one person giving spiritual companionship to another.

But beyond that, spiritual direction is reliant upon a theology of the Holy Spirit. The belief implicit in spiritual direction is that God's Spirit is alive and active in the world, constantly moving in the believer's life. The second premise is that believers who are experienced in life and faith and who are committed to spiritual disciplines themselves may be able to help others to notice the movements of the Spirit.

Most of the practices outlined in this book combat the noisiness of our world, and spiritual direction is no different. Because our lives are so quickly crowded with hockey games, band concerts, and family vacations, many of us need to schedule a time once or twice a month to meet with a spiritual director.

It will help to define spiritual direction by noting what it's *not:*

Spiritual direction is not psychotherapy nor is it an inexpensive substitute, although the disciplines are compatible and frequently share raw material. Spiritual direction is not pastoral counseling, nor is it to be confused with the mutuality of deep friendships.… [I]n this covenanted relationship the director has agreed to put himself aside so that his total attention can be focused on the person sitting in the other chair. What a gift to bring to another, the gift of disinterested, loving attention! [Guenther 3]

Although Jesus was surely "better" and "holier" than his disciples, the director-directee relationship attempts to mimic the Jesus-disciple relationship in a way that therapy, mentoring, and even pastoral counseling do not. Pastoral counseling most often takes place because of a crisis in the life of a parishioner or, in our case, a student. We help the person through the crisis, applying Scripture and accumulated wisdom to the issue at hand. Adults and students seeking spiritual direction, on the other hand, are looking for God, wanting to be held accountable in their prayer practices, and attempting to discern the Spirit in their lives. "In my view," says Eugene Peterson, "spiritual direction is a conversation in which the pastor takes the person seriously as a soul, as a creation of God for whom prayer is the most natural language." [Wood 24]

The *Catholic Encyclopedia* may say it best, under the assumption that all Christians are to strive for spiritual perfection, as both Jesus and Paul commended us to do, and a spiritual director's job is to guide the directee in that pursuit of perfection:

This striving after Christian perfection means the cultivation of certain virtues and watchfulness against faults and spiritual dangers. The knowledge of this constitutes the science of asceticism. The spiritual director must be well versed in this difficult science, as his advice is very necessary for such souls. For, as Cassian writes, "by no vice does the devil draw a monk headlong and bring him to death sooner than by persuading him to neglect the counsel of the Elders and trust to his own judgment and determination" (Conference of Abbot Moses). [www.newadvent.org]

Whereas the Orthodox and Catholic traditions emphasize a hierarchical model of spiritual direction that reflects their ecclesiology, an equally significant model is currently emerging in Protestant circles. In this model, the SD isn't necessarily older or more experienced than the directee. The director is seen primarily as a companion on the spiritual journey—one who is committed to taking time to listen to the spiritual goings-on of

PRACTICE

the directee. The underlying belief is that God communicates directly with his children. The director is not an expert who speaks for God, but one who helps others notice God's communication with them. "…[T]he sheep listen to his voice. He calls his own sheep by name and leads them out." [John 10:3]

One of my past SDs used this metaphor: "We're like two people sitting on a train; I'm in the aisle seat, you're in the window seat, and you are describing to me what you see." Beth Slevcove, the SD at Youth Specialties, likens it to a triangle where the bottom two corners represent the director and the directee and the top corner is the Holy Spirit, Jesus, or God (the *true* directors). "I sit on the same level as the directee as we together pay attention and listen to God." She compares this understanding of direction to Paul's statements that the church is the *body* of Christ, and the Lord is the *head* of this body.

In today's more team-oriented and lay-empowered churches, this latter model seems to make the most sense. While the SD is trained and professional, the relationship is one of equals listening, ultimately, for God's direction.

The growth and professionalization of spiritual direction in many ways parallels that of youth ministry. Since the 1960s, both professions have grown immensely with more schools offering programs and more literature being produced. In both cases, something that had been done more or less informally since the time of Jesus has become formalized in structure and training.

Nowadays, many Protestant spiritual directors are current or former pastors and others are laypeople, while Catholic SDs continue to be monks, nuns, and priests. The tradition of having a *starets* (Russian for 'spiritual father') is still common in the Orthodox church, but they can be difficult to find. Most spiritual directors have received formal training, either while in seminary or later, and they combine that with years of pastoral and spiritual experience. While some people like to follow the Orthodox tradition of an older, wiser SD, others value youth and the corresponding lack of predisposition in a younger SD.

You can find an SD in the Yellow Pages, but it's better to call a monastery in your vicinity—both Benedictine and Franciscan monasteries usually have SDs available. The Resource section in the back of this book has some links for finding an SD, including Youth Specialties' site, which specializes in finding SDs for youth workers.

Choosing an SD takes some patience. There should be a good vibe between the two of you, and you should have an inherent respect for your director's faith journey. Since spiritual direction isn't a forum for debating theology, it doesn't often matter if the director is from a different Christian tradition than you, but you may want to look for someone with whom you share an affinity. Presently, my SD is a former pastor who spent 16 years on the staff of a church very much like mine in size and location, so she has insight about maintaining a connection with God in a church like this—but someone else might want an SD from a totally different type of church than his own. Spiritual directors are trained in theology, Christian spirituality, church history, discernment, and listening skills. When looking for an SD, Beth suggests you seek out someone who is Christ-centered, discerning, compassionate, and honest about her journey of faith.

When I asked Beth to contribute the opening story for this chapter, she said that it's tough to talk about some particularly illuminating session with an SD because the sessions are rarely extraordinary. She's right—good spiritual direction is ordinary. Here's what Eugene Peterson says to the pastor/spiritual director about that ordinariness:

I have two basic definitions of spiritual direction. One is you show up and then you shut up. It's important that people have a place they can come to and know that you're going to be there with and for them. The other is that spiritual direction largely involves what you do when you don't think you're doing anything. You're not answering a question, and it doesn't seem like you're doing anything. It takes a lot of restraint and discipline for a pastor not to say anything, not to do anything. But the pastoral life is an ideal school for learning how to do it. [Wood 25]

Most SDs have hour-long sessions, and they may charge anywhere from $35 to $65 per meeting—once or twice a month is normal. Sessions often start with just a moment or two of chitchat and then silence. At first I thought, "I'm paying to sit in silence!" but then I came to find the silence an appropriate and peaceful way to begin. Most often the directee breaks the silence and the conversation flows from there. Most SDs don't take notes—another difference between SDs and therapists or pastoral counselors—but a good director will remember past dialogues and bring to light the thread of God's Spirit woven between them. In the end, each person's experience of spiritual direction is unique, a blessed chemistry between director and directee.

I also want to note that I've emphasized the currently popular model of hiring a professional SD. As Eugene Peterson has argued, this is also an oft-neglected role of the pastor, who is paid by the church. Finally, many of us have deep friendships that more easily fall into the category of Aelred's "spiritual friendship." Pastors and friends can both serve as spiritual directors, either formally or informally, but it seems to work best on a formal basis. Even with a friend, the more formal you can make it, the better: e.g., "We'll meet twice a year for two days each and take turns directing one another." Without the deliberate direction in the relationship, even the best Christian friends do not fall under either the ancient or modern definition of spiritual direction.

THOUGHTS FOR YOUTH MINISTRY

The first thing to say is that many of us…most of us…maybe all of us who engage in youth ministry should be under the care of a spiritual director, at least for a time. For all the reasons mentioned above, direction helps us grow in faith, stay committed to our disciplines, and gives us a few hours a month to be quiet and listen for God's voice in the voice of another. Just as a therapist should be in therapy so as to not take the burden of her clients into her own psyche, a youth pastor should have a spiritual director who won't let him internalize all of the spiritual conflicts of his students.

The next point is that you probably feel like a spiritual director for many of the students with whom you work, and indeed you do fill that role. But as you spend time with a director of your own, you'll become more aware of movements of the Spirit, and you might start to put more formal parameters around your direction-type relationships. If you've got a Confirmation or discipleship class, you might serve as an SD for students, or you might use adult mentors in the congregation to do so. In that case, bring in an experienced SD in your area to train your leaders in the basics of direction.

Finally, you might think of ways that students can act as spiritual companions to one another. Again, establish some formal boundaries and guidelines for the relationships, and provide training for the participants.

A FINAL WORD

Aelred of Rievaulx wrote this about Spiritual Friendship, and it is a beautiful picture of the heart of spiritual direction:

A friend is called a guardian of love or as some would have it, a guardian of the spirit itself. Since it is fitting that my friend be a guardian of our mutual love or the guardian of my own spirit so as to preserve all its secrets in faithful silence, let him, as far as he can, cure and endure such defects as he may observe in it; let him rejoice with his friend in his joys and weep with him in his sorrows and feel as his own all that his friend experiences. [Aelred 58]

Chapter 11

The Daily Office

Desire and pray always that God's will may be perfectly fulfilled in you.

Thomas à Kempis

In the Burgundy region of southern France, there's a village called Taizé. In 1940, Brother Roger arrived there, looking for a place to establish a brotherhood of Catholic and Protestant men who were committed to Christ, to each other, and to peace. The people of Taizé welcomed him warmly, and Brother Roger camped there on the outskirts of the village.

When I arrived there 62 years later, some things had changed dramatically, while others hadn't. Brother Roger was still there, surrounded by a group of brothers who have given up all worldly possessions, including even their inheritances, to the Taizé Community. They wear simple white cloaks, bound at the waist with a rope. But in the decades since Brother Roger founded the community, they've sent dozens of brothers out to serve in the world, written music that's used everywhere there are Christians, and become the major pilgrimage site for young Christians and seekers in Europe.

I made my first pilgrimage to Taizé in April 2002. I met a wide variety of people there: a youth pastor from Virginia with his family, a group of Catholic men in their 40s from Germany, a young woman from Holland. Lise, from Holland, had been at Taizé four times and had seen anywhere from about 60 pilgrims there in January to more than 7,000 in July.

I was one of about 1,000 pilgrims at Taizé on my visit. Located in a beautiful area of vineyards and rolling hills, the campus itself isn't particularly luxurious. Pilgrims are encouraged to bring tents, but there are barracks available for a few hundred people. The food is forgettable, stew and a small loaf of crusty bread served in plastic bowls. Dirt paths everywhere complete the rustic feeling of Taizé.

So I was baffled at first about the great attraction of this place—that is, until I went to evening prayers the first night. I got to the *Eglesia* a few minutes early, which was a good thing because hundreds were already gathered there. Seating is all on the floor, although some people get the few hundred kneeling benches scattered around. The church is dimly lit, and dozens of candles burn on the altar at the front.

Right up through the middle of the sanctuary, separated from the rest of the building by planters two feet tall, is a row of chairs and kneelers. One or two at a time, the brothers enter the sanctuary, walk up the middle, and take their places, praying before the service starts. At the appointed time, the bells outside start to ring and Brother Roger enters, walking with the aid of a cane and another brother. On a small screen, a digital read-out of the song number flashes, we find our place in the song-book, and everyone sings. And then I knew what Taizé is all about. The singing is unlike anything I've ever heard—all these people, most of them under 30, from different countries and different languages, united in song, and singing with gusto.

The songs are contemplative, sung in many different languages. They're simple tunes that are repeated for five minutes or more each. You never know when a song is going to end and I quit trying to guess pretty quickly. Sometimes after a song ends, there is complete silence—in a way you'd never think 1,000 people could be silent—for maybe 10 minutes. Once per day a Scripture passage is read, and once per day the Eucharist is served (holy bread is given to those who do not wish to receive communion).

And so I discovered that the morning, afternoon, and evening singing prayer services are the backbone, the lifeblood of Taizé. I cannot describe what happens in that sanctuary other than to say it's something mystical. When I talked to young people who were there for their second, third, or fourth times, they all talked about the worship, which they call 'prayer'. That's the thing that gets them back, and, indeed, it's the thing that has stuck with me and bounced around in my soul since I made my pilgrimage. It's that feeling that leads me to *know* that I'll go back.

HISTORY

The thrice daily service of prayer isn't unique to Taizé. In fact, the Daily Office (as it's typically called), is the common practice that links monasteries and clergy with laity around the world and through the centuries.

The people of God have long considered ordered prayers during the day a practice that pleases God, as the psalmist declares: "Seven times a day I praise you for your righteous laws." [Psalm 119:164] Although scholars don't know exactly when these seven times might have been (the perfection of the number "seven" in wisdom literature comes to mind), the Jews under Roman rule were influenced by their rulers. Without clocks being widely accessible, the bell in the forum of a Roman town rang to mark the passing of the day at 6 a.m. (the first hour), 9 a.m. (the third hour), etc. And so we read of Peter and John "going up to the temple at the time of prayer—at three in the afternoon (Greek: "the ninth hour")," [Acts 3:1] and, years later, Peter was on a rooftop in Joppa at noon (Greek: "the sixth hour"), when God spoke in his prayer and told him that all animals had been made clean. [Acts 10:9]

Along with the Lord's Supper, fixed-hour prayer is considered the oldest form of Christian spirituality. The Apostles used the psalms in their prayers (e.g., Acts 4:23-30), and the psalms remain the backbone of the Office today. The writer of the *Didache* (c. A.D. 60) commended the Lord's Prayer to be recited three times daily. Many of the Church Fathers of the second and third centuries taught the practice of morning and evening prayers, as well as prayers at the third, sixth, and ninth hours. In his Rule, Benedict formalized the Offices for his monks, which have continued in this basic form ever since:

Matins (from the Latin, 'of the morning'): The first office is held before dawn, keeping vigil for the day to come. Psalms 63 and 95 are often used, and silent prayer is at the heart of Matins.

Prime ('first'): The first of the "Little Hours," Prime is a reading of three psalms following an opening hymn. It's observed at 6 a.m.

Lauds ('praise'): Long have Christians seen the parallel between the rising of the sun at dawn and the return of Christ (thus most Catholic and Orthodox churches face east). Lauds is held at dawn, and its focus is the reading of Psalms 148-150 (the "Praise the Lord!" psalms).

Terce ('third'): The second of the "Little Hours," Terce (pronounced "terse") consists of three psalms, the Lord's Prayer, and a hymn. It's observed at 9 a.m.

Sext ('sixth'): The third of the "Little Hours," Sext consists of three psalms, the Lord's Prayer, and a hymn. It's observed at noon.

None ('ninth'): The fourth of the "Little Hours," None (pronounced like "known") consists of three psalms, the Lord's Prayer, and a hymn. It's observed at 3 p.m.

Vespers ('evening'): Held at dusk, Vespers (along with Lauds) is considered one of the two most important offices of the day. Vespers consists of five psalms, a short Scripture passage, a hymn, and it concludes reverently with the singing of the "Magnificat" (Mary's song from Luke 1:46-55).

Compline ('complete'): The prayers said at night before retiring, Compline (pronounced "cómp-line" or "cómp-lin") is traditionally Psalms 4, 91, and 134 and the "Nunc Dimittis" (Simeon's Song from Luke 2:29-32).

These are the traditional offices of the Western church as they have been practiced in Roman Catholicism. The prayer book for Anglicans and Episcopalians, *The Book of Common Prayer*, outlines the services of Morning Prayers (a combination of Matins and Lauds), a noon prayer (compressing the "Little Hours") and Evensong (a combination of Vespers and Compline).

Orthodox Christians practice three offices: *Hesperinos* ('Vespers'; the first office of the day since, like Jews, Orthodox believers start the new day at sunset), *Apodeipnon* (from the Greek, 'after supper'; like Compline), and *Orthros* ('dawn').

THEOLOGY

As is clear from the preceding history, fixed-hour prayer has been a part of the Christian tradition since its inception. As well as following the psalmist's example to praise God seven times daily, early practitioners were trying to follow Paul's exhortation to "pray without ceasing." [1 Thessalonians 5:17 NRSV] As Phyllis Tickle writes,

To accomplish this, [the Desert Fathers] devised the stratagem of having one group of monks waiting to commence the next office. The result was the introduction into Christian thinking of the concept of a continuous cascade of prayer before the throne of God.… Christians today, wherever they practice the discipline of fixed-hour prayer, frequently find themselves filled with a conscious awareness that they are handing their worship, at its final "Amen," on to other Christians in the next time zone. [Tickle (2001), ix]

Tickle makes another important point about the theology and focus of the Office. Whereas many prayers are rightly "petitionary or intercessory or valedictory or any number of other things," fixed-hour prayers always are and always have been exclusively an *offering to God*. Like the sacrifices of the Old Testament, "the Divine Hours are prayers of praise offered as a sacrifice of thanksgiving and faith to God and as a sweet-smelling incense of the human soul before the throne of God." [Tickle (2001), x]

The Office reorients the one who practices it, turning the gaze from the mundane experiences of daily life on earth, both good and bad, to the One who created it all. Of course, the constant reliance on the psalms throughout the Office inevitably does this. The psalms are cries to God, thanks to God, praise of God— they don't particularly lend themselves to theological reflection, but move the adherent to acknowledge that *we are the creatures and God is the Creator.*

Similarly, the traditional prayers attached to the Office reorient the pray-er. I am always moved by the final prayer for the evening from *The Book of Common Prayer:*

Keep watch, dear Lord, with those who work or watch or weep this night, and give your angels charge over those who sleep. Tend the sick, Lord Christ; give rest to the weary, bless the dying, soothe the suffering, pity the afflicted, shield the joyous; and all for your love's sake. Amen.

No matter what my frame of mind as I head to bed, no matter

PRACTICE

how well or badly things have gone for me on a given day, when I pray this prayer I'm automatically turned outward, to the needs of others, those I know and those I don't. And I'm reminded that in heaven sits a powerful and sovereign God who has all those who need him in the palm of his hand.

Think of the recent media coverage of faithful Muslims who stop five times daily—at work, at home, while traveling—and pray toward Mecca. This is a countercultural practice: to stop commerce, travel, conversation, even ministry(!)—to stop, for a short time, the advancement of an individual and by extension society, in order to make an offering to God. Our culture does not reward those of us who stop for God…but God does. God rewards the one who practices the Office with peace and with an intimacy of relationship that truly is the meaning of life down here.

Observing the Office is, obviously, a routine that takes an enormous amount of discipline. It's best if the practitioner doesn't begin by trying to keep seven hours a day! From the earliest days, prayer books have reflected a difference between religious (cloistered monks and nuns) and secular (parish priests and nuns) clergy. To be cloistered gives one the opportunity to stop as many times a day as the community determines for prayer.

While I was at the Sabbath Retreat, we had morning and evening prayers, about half an hour each. At Taizé there are three services daily, each lasting about 45 minutes, around which the whole life of the community revolves. For me, both Taizé and Sabbath were times of relative cloister, or retreat from the world. Meanwhile other resources take seriously the fact that most of us live in the secular world most of the time and our daily prayers will be personal and private.

Most prayer books are designed for the public observance of the Daily Office. You might find an Episcopalian, Anglican, Catholic, or Orthodox church near you that has morning and evening prayers. Some downtown churches have a daily noon prayer service for working people. But the fact is, fewer and

I'm in a Starbucks® in the shadow of Westminster Abbey. I woke this morning at 6:30 to begin morning prayers and the routine of the daily office. What freedom! What a difference from a "Quiet Time." The structure, the purpose(fulness), the direction. It seems that the office, and, by extenuation, the whole day, is on a line. It's like I'm actually "going somewhere" with my day.

I started reading *The Illumined Heart* this morning. Frederica Mathewes-Green has such a way of saying with simplicity, beauty, and poetic prose the universal desire of the human heart.

How poignant to read that, in every person, "there remains a melancholy awareness that each of us is still fundamentally alone, encapsulated in skin like a spaceman," as I sat alone in a B&B in London. I am truly alone here, separate from Julie and the kids, apart from my friends and my church. There is freedom in that, for good and ill, but there's also loneliness.

fewer churches, even of the ancient traditions, are keeping up with daily prayers. Our world is speeding up, people are busy, and, as Marva Dawn's recent book (*A Royal "Waste" of Time: The Splendor of Worshiping God and Being Church for the World*) has pointed out, worship is a "royal *waste* of time."

So if you want to experience the Office corporately, that is, with other people, you probably have two choices: 1) find a monastery or convent nearby where you can join in, or 2) develop a service of your own with a group of people, however small, who are similarly committed to it.

It is likely that most of us will observe the Office privately and alone. To do this, as I said, takes enormous discipline and commitment. I find that when I travel, I can easily and enthusiastically practice four offices daily: morning, noon, evening, and nighttime. However, when I'm home, it's a lot more difficult to separate myself from Julie and our two toddlers to go off and pray. Julie and I have experimented some with involving our children, but I imagine this will be easier as they get older. In the end, each of us must look at our lives and determine, realistically, which offices we can make a part of our lives.

There's been a recent publishing bonanza of daily prayer books; in addition to the old favorites, the Roman Catholic *Breviary* and the Anglican/Episcopalian *Book of Common Prayer*, there are Benedictine, Celtic, Franciscan, Reformed, and other types available (some of my favorites are in the bibliography). However, I can't imagine that there's a better resource than the three-volume *The Divine Hours* by Phyllis Tickle. She has compiled the best of many other resources, updated the archaic language, and put them in the most usable format imaginable. Using a book like this alleviates much of the frustration that can thwart a novice's attempts at keeping the Office.

THOUGHTS FOR YOUTH MINISTRY

The traditional evangelical practice of having a daily "quiet time" is definitely a form of fixed-hour prayer. And many of our students are quite good about having a "QT," or even praying in the morning and in the evening. Teaching them about the Office and giving them a prayer book, however, does something more. First of all, it links students to the history of the church—to imagine that you are praying a prayer that has been said by Christians for hundreds of years is a powerful thing!

Secondly, the Office links students with Christians around the world, especially when lectionary texts are included (as they are in many prayer books). In other words, millions of Christians around the world are reading the same psalm and the same gospel lesson as I am. Finally, if you can either find or fashion a prayer book that you, your volunteers, and all the students are using, a unity of purpose and prayer will develop among all of you.

And just imagine if a group of students at your local high school stopped every day for 10 minutes during the lunch period, pulled out a prayer book, and quietly prayed to God!

Practicing the Office corporately particularly lends itself to a retreat, camp, or mission trip. It's not hard to imagine replacing your normal chapel or "club" times at the fall retreat with three prayer services. Quiet, contemplative gatherings with ancient prayers, repetitive Scripture readings, and silence would definitely set a different tone for the retreat than the usual crazy chapel times.

It might look like this: upon waking up, silence is kept until breakfast. Before breakfast, morning prayers are held—students enter to silence or quiet music, sing a contemplative opening song, hear the psalm for the morning, sit in silence for 10 minutes, and sing a quiet closing song. Similar services are held before lunch (with a time for spoken prayers) and before bed (with communion). Silence is kept following Compline prayers. "Club" or the usual teaching time can either be forgone or slotted in the late afternoon. Then at the end of the weekend, students can be given a prayer book that follows the general outline of the prayer services from the weekend.

A FINAL WORD

Phyllis Tickle, compiler of *The Divine Hours,* writes the following:

Asking me why I keep the Offices is like asking me why I go to church. One, granted, is a place of bricks and mortar, but the other is a chapel of the heart, as powerful a place, albeit one of the spirit. The Offices open to me four times a day and call me to remember who owns time and why it is, as a part of creation. All that means really is that four times a day the watchmaker and I have conversation about the clock and my place as a nano-second in it. [www.thedivinehours.com]

Part III: Via Activa
Bodily Approaches to Spirituality

Chapter 12

The Labyrinth

Just as a ship without a helm is driven to and fro by the waves, so a careless man, who abandons his proper course, is tempted in countless ways.

Thomas à Kempis

Lizzy is currently in 11th grade. She wrote this as part of her confirmation paper last year:

At the start of the second semester of my freshman year in high school last January, things were at their worst for me. I had lost touch with God and couldn't get back on my feet. I felt as if there was no way to get out of my problems. Luckily, due to a mere "coincidence," I got right back on my feet again. This "coincidence" was the main turning point in my life and my faith. Here's what I'm talking about: In the middle of January, I had several downfalls. I am not going to mention any of those, except for one that I do need to mention. That is the fact that I started realizing that I was not being treated very fairly in my home. I no longer felt like the "A-honor-roll, never-gotten-in-serious-trouble-daughter" I had worked hard to be. I felt as if I was being treated as a servant, and mostly, as a delinquent drug-addicted rebel of a child, even though I wasn't!

Maybe that's going a bit overboard, but you get the idea. One Sunday night, I was just sitting on the couch and my sister asked if I wanted to go to PF that night. (PF is our high school youth group.) I said "sure, why not." I had nothing else to do, so I went. Boy, did I pick the night to go. The activity that evening was the "labyrinth." I was expecting to get maybe a little boost out of it, but not much. However, what I actually got was *much, much* more than that. I got answers and help to most of my questions, along with the insight to start a plan for a better life.

I had never seen nor participated in a labyrinth before, but I gave it a shot. As I walked, I talked to God about my problems at home, and asked him to help me get through it and figure out what to do. I also asked him to help me turn my life around and get my footing back so I could continue on my faith journey.

As I walked silently toward the center of the labyrinth, I felt myself getting closer to God. After I reached the center of the labyrinth, I was in tears. God had touched me and he was very present in that room with me that night. I felt him so close to me, it gave me the shivers. After PF was over, I went over and talked to Megan, a trusted leader. Well, I mostly cried and Megan talked to me. She prayed for me, that I would figure out what to do with my mom.

Looking back at the events following my labyrinth experience, I realize that God really did answer my prayers that night. He answered my questions and helped me through everything. That night was so powerful for me. I will never forget it.

HISTORY

Labyrinths of various shapes and sizes date back thousands of years: a labyrinthine rock carving in Sardinia dates to around 2500 B.C.; pottery from 1300 B.C. in Syria shows a labyrinth; a clay tablet in Greece from 1200 B.C. shows the design; and the remains of a labyrinth from around this time have been found at the top of Mt. Knossos, on the isle of Crete (especially interesting because legend has it that the ancient Trojans were remnants of the tribe of Benjamin, exiled after the rape and murder of the Levite's concubine, told in Judges 19-20).

A labyrinth is a pattern, first found on pottery. The type of labyrinth we are concerned with, however, is laid out on the ground for walking, and has a circuitous route to a center. Unlike a maze, there are no wrong turns; the path in is the same as the path out. "Labyrinths are unicursal. They have one well-defined path that leads us into the center and back out again. There are no tricks to it, no dead ends or cul-de-sacs, no intersecting paths." [Artress 51] The origin of the word is hotly debated—some believe that labyrinth comes from 'labrys,' the name of the ancient Minoan double-headed ax. (This is the shape formed between two back-to-back turns in a Roman-style pattern).

Labyrinthine designs are a part of almost every culture and religion, and they were incorporated into Christian art and architecture in the first centuries after Jesus. The earliest extant Christian labyrinth dates from 325 at a church in Algiers; at its center is a mosaic acrostic spelling *santa ecclesia*, 'holy church.'

In the Middle Ages, when pilgrimages to Jerusalem, Rome, and Santiago were becoming more dangerous because of the Crusades, the church ordained seven cathedrals in France as alternate pilgrimage sites. One of these was the cathedral at Chartres, the location of the best-maintained example of a labyrinth from that time. Although no literature mentioning the labyrinth from that period remains, it seems that to complete the pilgrimage to Chartres, a pilgrim would walk the route to the center of labyrinth, which is laid out in the floor, before proceeding to the altar to receive the Eucharist.

Because of its size, its beautifully symmetrical layout, and its importance in Christian history, the Chartres labyrinth has become the archetype for thousands of more recently constructed labyrinths. Laid in the floor between 1194 and 1220, the labyrinth at Chartres is of the 11-circuit design. That means 11 concentric circles surround the center circle, and the path meanders between the circuits. The turns, 10 of which are labryses, create four quadrants and a cruciform design when seen from above. The path turns seven times in each quadrant and six times along the entrance/exit path. The exterior of the labyrinth has 113 notches, or "lunations," which some believe form a lunar calendar used to set the date of Easter. The entire pattern is 42 feet in diameter.

At the center of the labyrinth is a circle outlined by six smaller circles. Some see in this a six-petaled flower, the rose being a symbol both of the Virgin Mary and of the Holy Spirit. The six petals can be understood to represent the six days of creation, and some walkers visit each petal, thanking God for what he created on each day. Others see seven circles (the six smaller and the one larger that binds them) as the intersection of heaven (the Trinity) and earth (the four directions).

In 1991, Lauren Artress, a pastor at Grace Episcopal Cathedral in San Francisco, went to Chartres to walk the labyrinth there—she had walked another labyrinth and was interested in introducing one in her own church. When she and her friends arrived, the medieval labyrinth was covered with chairs. Artress and her friends moved the chairs and, before they were told to put them back, had a chance to walk the 861-foot path to the center. [Artress 1–7]

Artress was deeply moved by the experience. Upon her return to San Francisco, her church painted an 11-circuit labyrinth on canvas for use at Grace Cathedral. The response was overwhelming. People lined up around the block for the semi-monthly openings. Veriditas, the organization she founded, was soon receiving requests from around the world to speak, write, and design more labyrinths. Veriditas has been on the forefront of a massive revival of labyrinth construction, sales, and training since the early 1990s. Every major city in North America now boasts numerous labyrinths, churches of every persuasion have incorporated them into worship, and institutions such as hospitals and seminaries have integrated them into their gardens.

An almost forgotten ancient and medieval spiritual tool is now arguably one of the most popular experiential devices in the church.

THEOLOGY

The labyrinth is a model or metaphor for life. The Christian life is often described as a pilgrimage of the faithful who are "in but not of the world." We progress down a path that's laid out by God, even though we rarely foresee its twists and turns, toward the eventual goal of union with Christ.

The labyrinth replicates our spiritual journey. We enter and follow a path, not knowing where it will take us, but knowing we will eventually arrive at the center. Sometimes the path leads inward toward the ultimate goal, only to lead outward again. We meet others along the path—some we meet face-to-face stepping aside to let them pass; some catch up to us and pass us from behind; others we pass along the way. At the center we rest, watch others, pray. Sometimes we stay in the center a long time; other times we leave quickly.

The point is, the labyrinth is a walking prayer:

The labyrinth is an archetype, a rich symbol that reaches into the depths of our human experience and hints at meaning that is both inescapable and inexhaustible. As a circle, it is a universal symbol of unity and wholeness. The labyrinth invites us to a journey within the sacred circle itself, offering a glimpse of the ineffable mystery of God. [Cannato 39]

Much has been written about the "sacred geometry" with labyrinth designs, most of which isn't particularly relevant to this study. There is, however, an inward-outward movement that also reflects the Christian life. "The walk inward becomes a journey of purification, meditation in the centre is compared to illumination, and the journey outward becomes union, a return to service in the world for the walking meditator who is refreshed and healed." [Mursell 338]

More is being written about the labyrinth every year, though at this time there exists no full-length study on the Christian theology of the labyrinth.

At Sabbath today we walked the labyrinth in community—there are about 70 of us total. Villa Maria has a great labyrinth—it's on the Chartres model, it's quite big, and it has a tree planted in the center. The paths are covered with wood chips and outlined with rocks. I'd walked it a few times since I've been here, but this was the time the whole group was introduced to it. At first I was jealous of the group experience—that is, I wanted to have the whole labyrinth to myself. I felt stupid, so I took my shoes off and walked barefoot so that it wouldn't be a totally comfortable experience for me. I used my chockti rope and found that at the pace I was walking, I completed a circuit of 100 Jesus Prayers and was reciting the Apostles' Creed as I entered the center. I must have walked more quickly on the way out, since I ended with about seven knots left on the rope.

My favorite thing about the labyrinth today was seeing the various postures that people used in the center—kneeling, standing, lying prostrate, arms in the air, arms across the chest (later I found out this is American Sign Language for "love"). Being toward the end of the week, I've gotten to know several of these people, and it was cool to see their different prayer postures, and see this embodiment of their prayer relationship with Christ.

PRACTICE

St. Augustine wrote that some problems can be "solved by walking" and the labyrinth is a tool to help facilitate this perambulatory prayer. Since virtually no literature exists explaining how medieval Christians used the labyrinth in their lives, all instruction on labyrinth use is recent and evolving. Jill Geffrion, a leader in the current labyrinth movement, has written of her early experiences of walking: "Two truths about labyrinth praying guided me through my pilgrimage and opened the door to many rich experiences. The first was a deep, intuitional knowing that there was no 'right' way to pray the labyrinth. The other was that God is very present in the midst of labyrinth praying." [Geffrion (1999) xiii]

One of the most common ways to pray the labyrinth is to ask God a question upon entering and then to listen for his answer. Another method is to pray for yourself on the way in, stop to simply experience God's love in the center, and pray for others on the way out (or vice versa). One of the first times I walked a labyrinth, I asked God what he needed to tell me; by the time I was in the center, I was convicted that I needed to spend more time praying for the kids in the youth group, and I spent the way out doing just that.

It can also be meaningful to recite the Lord's Prayer, liturgical prayers, or psalms while walking:

It was during this first walk that I began to reflect on Psalm 139. Walking the labyrinth felt like walking around in the shoes of the psalmist who sang of the One who searches our hearts and knows us better than we know ourselves. The labyrinth enabled me to be immersed in the psalm, while the psalm rendered the labyrinth a deeply moving experience of prayer. [Cannato 40]

Finding a labyrinth is becoming increasingly less difficult. Grace Cathedral hosts a worldwide labyrinth locator on its Web site and many local newspapers have done stories highlighting the labyrinths in their vicinity. Most outdoor labyrinths are open all the time, while indoor labyrinths usually have posted hours. It's also possible to purchase a canvas labyrinth, or to order a plan for instructions to make one.

THOUGHTS FOR YOUTH MINISTRY

A whole different kind of labyrinth has been pioneered by Jonny Baker and the Youth for Christ staff in London. Baker's interactive, multimedia labyrinth has 11 stations. Students are given a CD player and headphones and a disembodied voice leads the pray-er through the stations with narration that is recorded over ambient music.

The first five stations on the path are journey inward, noise, letting go, hurts, and distractions. At the center is "Holy Space," at which students are told to "let God love you." On the way out, the stations are outward journey, self, planet, others, and impressions. The stations incorporate computers, televisions, and artwork to complete the multisensory experience.

YFC's labyrinth is touring cathedrals in the U.K. You can also try it at the Youth Specialties Conventions or order a kit to make your own from Group Publishing.

Whether you take students to a labyrinth in your area or bring a canvas labyrinth into your setting, the more traditional Chartres-style labyrinth is highly accessible for students and easy to facilitate. Bearing some guidelines in mind (e.g., this is a prayer; there's no right or wrong way to pray this prayer), you can easily make this powerful tool available to your students.

When visiting a public labyrinth, be respectful of the people who have opened the labyrinth and of the others who might be walking it when you visit. Allow students the *option* of walking—some people have a powerful experience sitting along the edge and watching others walk. Don't take pictures or video unless you've gotten permission (just as you wouldn't walk into a church and start videotaping its worship). And allow the students as much time as they need to complete the journey.

Please, walk a labyrinth a few times yourself before you bring students to one—as with any of these spiritual practices, investigate them yourself before laying them on your students.

A FINAL WORD

From Jonny Baker in London:

Labyrinth plays fantastically well into the culture at the moment. It invites people into an experience, and while they are guided through the Labyrinth they aren't told how to react or what to think. [Adams 21]

Chapter 13

Stations of the Cross

If you cannot contemplate high and heavenly things, take refuge in the Passion of Christ, and love to dwell within his Sacred Wounds. For if you devoutly seek the Wounds of Jesus and the precious marks of his Passion, you will find great strength in all troubles.

Thomas à Kempis

Jess is a freshman in high school:

Christianity is full of contradictions and loopholes. On the first hand, it's okay to discipline your child, but then there's that pesky commandment about treating your neighbor as you would be treated that has stemmed the golden rule of elementary schools. But this isn't about my views of Christianity, it's about the chronology of Jesus' last 30 or so hours alive on this planet before Pontius Pilate nailed him to a large wooden cross. The image of Jesus stretched out on the cross is more or less central to Christianity.

This brings me to my father. My father is somewhat an atheist, but he grew up in the Catholic church. I believe he was a spirited child who was turned off at some point by the church. But he still likes to talk to me about my faith, even though he had no opinion about the Stations of the Cross when I asked him.

Our church is very different from a Catholic church. I enjoy the services, more or less, because they seem so much more relaxed than others. The band playing songs in a psuedo-contemporary fashion, the pastors talking in analogies about Christian experiences, and the closing prayer. All enjoyable. But that's besides the point. This is all pointing toward our Bible study. It consisted of the four of us. Tim, the youth minister, Nick, Erik, and me. I think I suggested the field trip to the Basilica one day after reading about its architecture. It was to be a journey of exploration to me, not faith. So, after school one day, we all climbed into Tim's car on our way to the Basilica. The 15-minute ride down there was like any other car trip, but music was missing (a minor detail). We arrived there and clambered out. We all entered the giant double wooden doors quietly, as to not disturb God in his hour of studies. I glanced around the giant hall, in awe at the beautiful architecture (better than the article) and the stained glass windows depicting certain saints. It was dimly lit inside, the only light filtering in through the windows and candles burning. We all explored the church, trying not to disturb whatever it was not wanting to be disturbed until I glanced at a copper print bolted to the wall. After some speculation, I discovered it, in fact, depicted the Stations of the Cross.

I didn't look at all of them, only hopped from one to the next. I bet if it were a service, and I was required, too, I would've feigned a certain interest, I'm that devoted. But that doesn't mean it didn't have any value to me. I thought the copper prints were beautiful in and of themselves, looking the way aged copper does to me, demanding a certain amount of respect and recognition for the copper worker who was responsible for their production. I skitted around, glancing at one, then hopping to another, trying to understand the dashes at the bottom of each one. I think it's neat how Jesus and certain other holy figures are depicted with those circles around their heads, a type of holy aura.

A few weeks after our trip, the Stations of the Cross were set up at JPF, a program for Christian youths at our church. I always enjoy this one. I find it very inspiring to see others' reactions to the pieces of cardboard set up, depicting Jesus' public disgrace, his painful journey to where he would ultimately meet his final hours. Seeing the other kids, some with their heads bowed in silent prayer, others reading or just looking, and the less interested pretending to care. There's something about Jesus' words when the Roman soldiers were beating him, the phrase "Forgive them father, for they know not what they do"—very humbling how one man could sacrifice so much.

This all connects back to my personal faith. I have questions, I have my doubts, but they're not enough to lose faith entirely. Sometimes in church, I feign my interest, but other discussions and sermons I find very interesting, and I pay close attention to them. Sometimes it's difficult to believe, which comes back to the age-old question "why does God let bad things happen if he's so mighty" which there may never be an answer to (and if there is, I haven't heard it yet, or have but have already forgotten). But hey, I've made my decision, and that's all I need right now.

HISTORY

From the earliest days of the church, Christians have journeyed to Jerusalem to retrace Jesus' steps as he carried his cross from Pilate's house to Golgotha. According to tradition, this path, which has become known as the *Via Dolorosa* ('Way of Sorrow') and the *Via Crucis* ('Way of the Cross'), was walked often by Jesus' mother, Mary, after his death. Jerome (c.325-420), the famous saint who translated the Bible into Latin, wrote of the hundreds of pilgrims in Jerusalem who walked this devotional path in his day.

The route Jesus walked quickly became well known, and informal markers demarcated the places he started, received his cross, where he stopped and fell, met his mother, and was assisted by Simon of Cyrene. Pilgrims then arrived at the hill known as the "Place of the Skull" where Jesus was stripped of his garments and crucified. By the Middle Ages, visitors to Jerusalem were taken on this *Via Sacra* ('Sacred Way') by guides. And in other cities around Europe, facsimiles of this *Via Sacra* were developed so that pilgrims could walk this journey with Jesus more often than once in a lifetime. One of the first of these was in Bologna, Italy, where a collection of chapels was built to replicate the important pilgrimage sites in Jerusalem.

In 1342, the holy places in Jerusalem were placed under the guardianship of the Franciscan Order. A 15th-century English pilgrim, William Wey, was the first to write about the practice of stopping along the route to pray and meditate on Jesus' journey to crucifixion. By the turn of the 16th century, replicas of the *Via Dolorosa* were popping up all over Italy, Spain, and Germany, many replicating the exact route in Jerusalem, measured off in paces.

The early literature has no set number of stations; they vary from seven to 37. In the 17th century when the 14 stations became formalized, Jerusalem was in the hands of the Turks, and it was illegal to stop along the route, uncover your head, and pray. So it seems most likely that the 14 stations we now know were formalized around Europe instead of in Jerusalem. When the Roman Catholic church connected indulgences to the practice of praying the Stations in the late 17th century, they became very popular, and today most Catholic sanctuaries have the 14 stations around the walls.

Some of the artwork connected with the Stations is world renowned, but most churches simply have 14 crosses on the walls, each with a Roman numeral over the top signifying the

THEOLOGY

station. Since no prescribed prayer is attached to the practice of the Stations, beautiful prayers for each station abound in prayer books, on Web sites, and in Catholic and Protestant liturgies.

The Stations are most often practiced during Lent and especially during Holy Week. Many churches hold special services around the Stations on Good Friday. The most famous set of stations may be around the Colosseum in Rome; every Friday a Franciscan Friar leads pilgrims through these stations, and on Good Friday, the Pope walks them.

Very recently, some churches have added a 15th station, celebrating Christ's resurrection, but all agree that this station is not to be observed during Lent.

"If any want to be my followers, let them deny themselves and take up their cross and follow me." [Matthew 16:24, Mark 8:34, Luke 9:23 (NRSV)] In no uncertain terms Jesus makes his claim on our lives in all three synoptic gospels. Christians are to follow him to the cross and to follow him on the *Via Crucis*, the way of the cross. Jesus' entire life, and especially his three-year ministry, can be seen as part of this road, for every miracle he performed, every parable he told, and every invective he unleashed on the Pharisees took him one step closer to his crucifixion.

When he entered Jerusalem on Palm Sunday, the segment of that road he traveled was paved with cloaks and tree branches. By Friday of that week, it was paved with stones spattered with drops of blood from his forehead. Luke records the beginning of Jesus' march to the cross, shuffled between Pilate and Herod that morning:

So Pilate decided to grant their demand. He released the man who had been thrown into prison for insurrection and murder, the one they asked for, and surrendered Jesus to their will. As they led him away, they seized Simon from Cyrene, who was on his way in from the country, and put the cross on him and made him carry it behind Jesus. A large number of people followed him, including women who mourned and wailed for him. Jesus turned and said to them, "Daughters of Jerusalem, do not weep for me; weep for yourselves and for your children." [Luke 23:24-28]

The 14 Stations of the Cross trace Jesus' path from Pilate's house to Golgotha to his tomb, mixing some events that we find in Scripture with some that come to us via the tradition of the church. Cardinal John Henry Newman (1801-1890) was a renowned churchman who wrote short and long reflections on the Stations. Here are reflections on the Stations that we wrote and recorded on a CD for our students, influenced by Newman's writings:

You are about to walk along the Way of the Cross, also called the *Via Dolorosa* or the Road of Sorrow. The Way of the Cross traces the journey taken by Jesus on the last day of his earthly life. Over 15 stations, you will travel with Jesus from the moment he was condemned to death to the victorious moment of his resurrection. This path has been walked by millions of Christians over 2,000 years. May God bless you on your journey.

Station One: Jesus Is Condemned to Death

The holy, just, and true Son of God was judged by sinners and sentenced to die. Judas betrayed him, the crowd shouted for his death, and Pilate sentenced him. In beginning this road to the cross, Jesus becomes one with everyone who has ever suffered, everyone who has ever bled or been scorned or been unfairly punished. He becomes one with you and me. The very creator of the universe experiences the ultimate human suffering.

O Lord, may I be moved by this journey. May I make this journey with you and you with me. Do not leave me alone on this way, even though your own followers abandoned you at your hour of need. We adore you, O Christ, and we bless you, because by your holy cross you have redeemed the world. Amen.

Station Two: Jesus Receives His Cross

Jesus carries the weight of his own cross on his shoulders, and upon that cross is heaped the weight of all of our sins. *My sins cost him this humiliation.* He became a human being so he could enter into our joy and our pain, and so, ultimately, he could take our sins away. And now the weight of those sins crushes down on him with every step.

O Lord God Almighty, you bear the weight of the whole world— you bore the weight of all my sins, and, though they wearied you, you carried them all the way to your death. We adore you, O Christ, and we bless you, because by your holy cross you have redeemed the world. Amen.

Station Three: Jesus Falls under the Weight of the Cross for the First Time

Suddenly, Jesus falls. The weight of the cross is too much. He cannot bear it. He is on the ground, and he knows what it is to feel defeated, weak, unable to go on. And yet, he must go on. The soldiers pick him up and force him to continue.

O dear Lord, by this, your first fall, raise me out of sin, I who have so miserably fallen under its power. Give me strength to continue my journey, even when I feel that I can't go on. We adore you, O Christ, and we bless you, because by your holy cross you have redeemed the world. Amen.

Station Four: Jesus Meets His Mother

What must it be like to see your mother as you are walking to your own execution? Mary gave birth to this boy, she brought him as an infant into the temple, she lifted him up in her arms when the wise men came to adore him. She fled with him to Egypt, she took him up to Jerusalem when he was 12 years old. He lived with her at Nazareth for 30 years. She was with him at the marriage feast. Even when he left her to preach, she hovered about him. And now she's there to give him comfort at the hour of his death.

Dear Jesus, what did you think when you saw your mother there? Give me the steadfast faith she had, and the courage to stay by your side, even when all others have fled. We adore you, O Christ, and we bless you, because by your holy cross you have redeemed the world. Amen.

Station Five: Simon of Cyrene Helps Jesus to Carry the Cross

Jesus could have carried the cross alone, but he allowed a man named Simon to help him. Just as he could feed the hungry and clothe the naked and build homes for the homeless without me…but he does not. Instead, he relies on me to aid him, to help him build the kingdom, to help him carry the cross.

Dear Lord, teach me to suffer with you, make it pleasant for me to suffer for your sake. And when my time comes to help you bear the cross, give me the courage and strength of Simon to step forward and do my part. We adore you, O Christ, and we bless you, because by your holy cross you have redeemed the world. Amen.

Station Six: The Face of Jesus Is Wiped by Veronica

As Jesus walks this sorrowful journey, the blood that drips from the crown of thorns on his head mixes with the spit of those who mock him. Out of the crowd comes a compassionate friend, Veronica, who wipes the spit, blood, and sweat from his face. Only for a moment, Jesus feels some relief.

O Lord God, Veronica is an example to me of someone who does the simple, compassionate act in a time of need. Remind me that it's not always the big things that matter, but often the smallest that can have an impact. We adore you, O Christ, and we bless you, because by your holy cross you have redeemed the world. Amen.

Station Seven: Jesus Falls a Second Time

The weight is too much and Jesus falls again. His knees scrape on the road, and his face is pushed into the dirt. Maybe he's reminded that "from dust you came and to dust you shall return." Maybe he catches his breath for a moment before the soldiers force him back to his feet.

King of the Universe, you tasted the dirt as the heavy wood of the cross fell on top of you. I am again shocked at the weight of my own sin, and I am humbled that you would suffer such humiliation for me. We adore you, O Christ, and we bless you, because by your holy cross you have redeemed the world. Amen.

Station Eight: The Women of Jerusalem Mourn for Our Lord

Jesus broke so many barriers for his day: he touched lepers, he healed on the Sabbath, and he spoke to women in public. Jesus ignored traditions that were oppressive, and he stood up to the authorities who challenged him. And now the women of Jerusalem show their gratitude by meeting Jesus along the way and crying over his fate. Earlier, Jesus prophesied that the women of Jerusalem would weep for him, and now that prophecy is fulfilled.

O Jesus, the cross is so commonplace in our world: around necks, hanging on walls, in cemeteries. Remind me what an awful torture you had to endure, so that I, too, might weep over your death when I see a cross. We adore you, O Christ, and we bless you, because by your holy cross you have redeemed the world. Amen.

Station Nine: Jesus Falls a Third Time

Utterly broken and devastated, Jesus falls again. This time, even the soldiers know that he can't rise by his own power. They roughly grab the Son of God and half-drag, half-push him up the rest of the hill. Is the cross getting heavier? Is Jesus getting weaker? The life that has raised the dead, healed the lame, and given sight to the blind is draining from him.

O Jesus, only begotten Son of God, the Word made flesh, I adore with fear and trembling and deep thankfulness your awful humiliation. The fact that you allowed yourself to be so disgraced brings me to my knees. We adore you, O Christ, and we bless you, because by your holy cross you have redeemed the world. Amen.

Station Ten: Jesus Is Stripped of His Garments

Jesus' life was a life of poverty—he gave up all earthly possessions to preach the gospel of Good News. Now, even the cloak he wears is violently stripped from him, tearing open the whip wounds on his back. As if the indignity of crucifixion weren't enough, Jesus now stands naked before the crowd.

Lord Jesus, you withstood the mocking and derision heaped upon you, and you faced your fate with dignity. May I, too, stand with courage when all is stripped from me. We adore you, O Christ, and we bless you, because by your holy cross you have redeemed the world. Amen.

Station Eleven: Jesus Is Nailed to the Cross

Huge, sharp spikes are hammered through Jesus' wrists and feet—he almost loses consciousness with each swing of the hammer. Now he is raised up and the cross drops with a thud into a hole in the ground. Jesus' weight hangs on those spikes, and to breathe he has to pull himself up on the nails. A sponge with vinegar is stuck in his mouth, and soldiers below him gamble for his clothes, even as the blood, breath, and life drain from his body.

O Jesus, dear Jesus, though you never sinned, you hang there on the cross. I should be there, not you. You hang there in my place. We adore you, O Christ, and we bless you, because by your holy cross you have redeemed the world. Amen.

Station Twelve: Jesus Dies upon the Cross

Every breath is a struggle. Wheezing, Jesus whispers in a voice barely audible, "Father, into your hands I commend my spirit." One more gasping breath, then his head drops, and it is finished. A soldier jams a spear between his ribs as a test, and the blood and water that issue forth show conclusively that the Savior of the world is indeed dead. The price is paid, and we are redeemed.

Father in Heaven, what did you feel as your son died upon that cruel piece of wood? Holy Spirit, did you grieve when your Divine Brother was taken from you? We adore you, O Christ, and we bless you, because by your holy cross you have redeemed the world. Amen.

Station Thirteen: Jesus Is Laid in the Arms of His Mother

Jesus hasn't been held in his mother's arms since he was a baby, but now his lifeless body is taken down from the cross and laid across her lap. What tears she cries! Her 33-year-old son, the Messiah, crusted with blood, naked, and dead is beyond her help, so she, too, is helpless.

Father God, did you weep to see the once naïve, teenage girl now, three decades later hold the dead body of her son…of your son? We adore you, O Christ, and we bless you, because by your holy cross you have redeemed the world. Amen.

Station Fourteen: Jesus Is Laid in the Tomb

At the very moment that Jesus was closest to his eternal glory, he seemed to be farthest from it. His body was placed in a stone-cold tomb, sealed with a massive rock, guarded by Roman soldiers. Death is so very final.

Give me the trust, O Christ, that your plans are higher than mine. For even when all seems lost, you're still at work. Death is not the final word for you, Son of Life. We adore you, O Christ, and we bless you, because by your holy cross you have redeemed the world. Amen.

Station Fifteen: The Tomb Is Empty

Sunday morning, Easter—the stone is rolled away, the tomb is empty except for some burial clothes. First the women find it this way, and soon after the disciples come to investigate. It truly is empty. The word goes forth: He is risen! He is risen, indeed! Death could not win, the tomb does not have the victory. Jesus Christ is stronger even than death!

My heart rejoices, Jesus, that the tomb could not hold you. You burst forth with new life, and you give me new life. I accept the gift you've given me—help me never to take it for granted! We adore you, O Christ, and we bless you, because by your holy cross you have redeemed the world! Amen.

You have now walked with Jesus, from Pilate's house, along the Via Dolorosa, to the top of Mt. Calvary. You have seen him crucified, dead, and laid in a tomb. And, finally, you have visited his empty tomb, so you know that his victory is complete. Now what? Will it change you? Will you respond to this ultimate gift given on your behalf?

That's up to you. Whatever you choose, may God bless you on your journey. He loves you more than you could ever imagine.

Peace.

Making the Stations has never been an intellectual exercise, but a spiritual and emotional one. Nor is it a historical act, as we see in Henri Nouwen's prayer for the Stations:

Dear Jesus,

You once were condemned; you are still being condemned. You once carried your cross; you are still carrying your cross. You once died; you are dying still. You once rose from the dead; you are still rising from the dead. [Nouwen (1990) 97]

At his Last Supper, Jesus washed his disciples' feet and, presumably talking about his entire life and ministry, said, "I have set an example that you should do as I have done to you." [John 13:15] To pray the Stations is to follow that example, meditating on the suffering Jesus experienced, the suffering we encounter, and the suffering throughout the world.

PRACTICE

The most common way to practice the Stations is to go to a church that has them around the walls, like Jess and his small group did. Most Roman Catholic churches have the Stations, and many monasteries have them outdoors along a prayer path.

Many churches host a "Living Stations of the Cross" during Holy Week. In the Living Stations, participants gather in small groups. After an introduction by their host, they are led from station to station. At each station, a responsive liturgy is read while actors stand still in a montage of the particular scene. Between stations, the group sings a meditative chorus (Taizé songs work well for this).

Here are three examples from a setting of Cursillo's "Living Stations" that we've used (there are seven stations in this setting):

Introduction

Leader: Paul said that we who have been baptized into Jesus have been joined to his suffering and his death and his resurrection. As we make these Stations of the Cross, the steps along the path Jesus took from his conviction to his crucifixion, know that each of us makes this journey with him. Let us pray:

People: Lord Jesus, the curtain is now about to go up on the awful drama of your love—a drama which we cannot forget, a drama of a love that will not forget us. And as we hear your words, "Take up your cross daily and follow me," some of us shudder to let those words come too close, lest the burden be too great and its shame too bitter. If we could only see that your command to follow you to Calvary is not just an iron law of cruel fate, but a condition of everlasting happiness—maybe then we could better make the journey.

Christ Speaks: These steps you are now about to pass through, you do not take alone. I walk with you. Though you are you and I am I, yet we are truly one—one in Christ. You, my brother, my sister, were baptized into me, joined to me, marked with the cross of Christ forever! And therefore my Way of the Cross two thousand years ago and your "way" now are also one. But note this difference: my life was incomplete until it was crowned by my death—your journey will only be complete when you have let me crown it with my life!

Station Two: Jesus Receives His Cross

Christ Speaks: This cross, this chunk of tree—this is what my

Father chose for me. The crosses you bear are largely the products of your daily lives, are they not? And yet my Father chose them for you, too. Receive them from his hands. Take heart, my brother, my sister: I will not let your burdens grow one ounce too heavy for your strength.

People: We know, Lord, how crosses are made. Your will is the timber that points up; ours is the one which crosses it. When we place our will against yours, we make the cross. Grant that we may make no more crosses for you, but that we might place our will alongside yours to make a yoke that will always be a burden fit to carry. Amen.

Station Five: Simon of Cyrene Helps Jesus to Carry the Cross

Christ Speaks: My strength is gone—I can no longer bear the cross alone. And so the soldiers make Simon give me aid. This Simon is like you, my brother, my sister. Give me your strength. Each time you lift some burden from someone's back, you lift as with your very hand the awful weight of the cross which crushes me.

People: Lord, help me to realize that every time I wipe a dish, pick up an object off the floor, assist another in some small task, or give someone preference in traffic or at the store—each time I feed the hungry, clothe the naked, teach the ignorant, or lend my hand in any way—it matters not to whom, my name is Simon. And the kindness I extend to them, I really give to you. Amen.

Another form of the Living Stations takes place on a stage or at the front of a sanctuary. Again, actors pose in the position of the scene and a responsive reading is read. Between scenes, the sanctuary is darkened, and a song is chanted or silence is kept.

A FINAL WORD

Thomas Merton, possibly the most celebrated monk of the 20th century, wrote this about the eve of his decision to enter the monastery:

The Retreat Master, in one of his conferences, told us a long story of a man who had once come to Gethsemani [Abbey], and who had not been able to make up his mind to become a monk, and had fought and prayed about it for days. Finally, went the story, he had made the Stations of the Cross, and at the final station had prayed fervently to be allowed the grace of dying in the Order.

"You know," said the Retreat Master, "they say that no petition you ask at the fourteenth station is ever refused."

In any case, this man finished his prayer, and went back to his room and in an hour or so he collapsed, and they just had time to receive his request for admission to the Order when he died.

He lies buried in the monks' cemetery, in the oblate's habit.

And so, the last thing I did before leaving Gethsemani, was to do the Stations of the Cross, and to ask, with my heart in my throat, at the fourteenth station, for the grace of a vocation to the Trappists, if it were pleasing to God. [Merton (1948) 363-364]

Chapter 14
Pilgrimage

Keep yourself a stranger and pilgrim upon this earth, to whom the affairs of this world are of no concern. Keep your heart free and lifted up to God, for here you have no abiding city.

Thomas à Kempis

Will Penner is Director of Youth Ministries at East Brentwood Presbyterian Church in Nashville, Tennessee, and editor of *Youthworker*, a contemporary journal for youth ministry. He wrote this about a recent trip his youth group took:

Two weeks after the September 11, 2001 terrorist attacks, we decided to forego plans for a foreign mission trip the following summer in favor of one to New York City. We wanted to visit Ground Zero, and we wanted to see if there would be anything we could do to help.

By the time we arrived, most of the work had already been done. A gaping hole remained where less than a year before the twin towers had stood. We'd originally planned on this being a mission trip to help others; it became much more of a pilgrimage that transformed us.

Along the fence at a church nearby are posted thousands upon thousands of letters, pictures, paintings, prayers, and other memorabilia sent and brought by the countless other pilgrims in memory of the innocent lives lost. We'd seen this on the news, on the Web, and in PowerPoint® presentations; we'd talked about it with family, with friends, in class, and at church.

But nothing compared to what it was like to be physically present in Manhattan.

We also spent time in Washington, D.C. on the way back to Nashville, and we were awestruck by the rows upon rows of graves, especially those marked "unknown," at Arlington National Cemetery. Additionally, the Vietnam memorial was strewn with more than 68,000 names of those who died there. They were like permanent scars, the evidence of the horrifying deaths suffered by soldiers hoping to preserve our freedom.

It was only natural for our conversations in the vans to turn to themes of life and death, justice and terror, trust and betrayal. We talked with hushed voices about the willing sacrifices made by soldiers and rescue workers, the unanticipated deaths of office workers and children, and of the cries of mothers and fathers and children of victims.

And we will never be the same.

Abbey is one of the students in Will's youth group:

The trip was amazing. If you go through your whole life and are never trapped in a van for 18 hours with 20 teenagers, then you are really missing out. It's crazy to think about all the laughs, stories, and discussions the van ride alone brought out in every youth (and adult) on the trip. We got lost, had car trouble, and messed up lodging reservations, but it was totally worth it.

We worked in a busy soup kitchen in Manhattan, painted a mosque in the Bronx, and did some touristy stuff, like the Empire State Building and Broadway. We ate our first slice of New York City pizza...very cool. And we had the very moving experience of visiting Ground Zero—an absolutely unforgettable moment.

I was reminded of just how truly blessed I am to have a home, food, and clothes to wear. I felt grief over the lives lost by the terrorism a year ago. I got to know my friends—the youth and adults—better than I ever imagined, and I got to know myself better, too. There will always be a special bond among those of us who went on that pilgrimage last summer.

HISTORY

The Bible is replete with archetypes for pilgrimage: Abram and Sarai left their homeland at God's command; Moses and the Israelites wandered for 40 years, following God toward their promised homeland; Jesus was, in many ways, a pilgrim during his entire three-year ministry, constantly moving from place to place; Paul undertook three missionary journeys to far-off lands, and other Apostles followed his example. Indeed, as we'll explore in the Theology section below, all of life east of Eden can be considered a pilgrimage.

And just as the New Testament states repeatedly, followers of Christ are "strangers and pilgrims on the earth." [Hebrews 11:13 NRSV] *Pilgrim* comes from the Latin word for 'resident alien,' also meaning to wander over a great distance, and pilgrimage has always upheld those two ideals: wandering and distance. Though the wandering is not aimless—it's pointed toward a goal—the wanderer spends a majority of the journey in a foreign land. And the greater the distance, the more admirable the journey.

After the Roman Emperor Constantine converted to Christianity and made it a legal religion in the Empire in 313, his saintly mother Helena made a famous pilgrimage to Jerusalem in 326. There she purportedly gathered dozens of sacred relics, most notably the cross on which Jesus was crucified, and brought them back to Rome. Within two years, her journey's fame spread, and pilgrims were setting off from all over Italy to visit the Holy Land.

The first guidebooks for such pilgrims were composed in the same century and they record much information both about the journey and about the traditions of Christian worship in Jerusalem at the time. The most famous and most complete of these is the *Peregrinatio Egeriae*, (the *Pilgrimage of Egeria*), which was written in 385 and discovered in Italy in 1884. Egeria seems to have been a nun or abbess who visited all of the major biblical sites in the Holy Land over three years, recording in detail what she saw.

Jerusalem was, and still remains, the primary pilgrimage site for Christians. Soon after Constantine's decree, churches were built over many of the sacred spots from Jesus' life and passion. Egeria describes visits to many of these spots during Holy Week, and her descriptions seem to show the beginnings of the Stations of the Cross.

Next in the hierarchy of pilgrimage sites was Rome, being the burial spot of the preeminent Apostles Peter and Paul. Constantine commissioned basilicas to be built over each of their tombs, and both structures had to be enlarged frequently to accommodate the crushing number of pilgrims.

In the early Middle Ages, Santiago de Compostela in Spain began to rise in prominence; between the 11th and 13th centuries it was by far the most popular of pilgrimage destinations. Tradition held that before he was beheaded in Jerusalem in A.D. 44, the Apostle James the Greater (brother of John, Son of Thunder) went on a missionary journey to Spain. Further, popular belief held that his remains returned to Spain, either miraculously or brought by a king, and were interred in Santiago (Spanish for 'Saint James'). An enormous cathedral was built over James' supposed burial spot and thousands upon thousands of pilgrims visited the shrine.

Pilgrims to Santiago and other shrines were distinguished by their garb: as well as sturdy shoes and a deerskin coat, all pilgrims carried a staff (*bordón*) and a bag (*escarcela*) and wore a patch. The staff was four to five feet long with an iron tip at one end and was useful for fighting off wild animals and for balancing through tricky river and mountain crossings. But, more importantly, "it was credited with chasing the devil away, and it stood for the *lignum crucis*, the Wood of the Cross." [Melczer 57] The bag was a trapezoid-shaped deerskin satchel, wider at the base than the top. "The *escarcela* had to be narrow and flat to remind the pilgrim to rely on the Great Provider alone instead of on his own provisions, it had to be always open in order to give and receive, and it had to be made of animal skin to evoke the mortifications of the flesh." [Melczer 58]

The patch served a dual purpose. First of all, it apparently granted the pilgrim safe passage through all lands by the authority of the church, as pilgrimages were always very dangerous. And the specific patch denoted the pilgrim's destination: two crossed palm leaves for Jerusalem, two keys (as given to St. Peter) for Rome, and a scallop shell for Santiago (the shell represents the open hand of one who freely gives and receives, and shells are collected on the beach outside Santiago). So important were these items that many exhumed medieval graves hold their denizens buried with a staff and scallop shells.

The pilgrimage was an arduous journey. For one who lived in France, the round trip to Santiago took about six months, and it was close to a year's journey for someone from northern Germany. The trail was pocked with treacherous mountain passes, unscrupulous ferry boat operators, and bandits posing as fellow pilgrims. On the other hand, monasteries and hospices were built along the route, offering pilgrims a warm meal and a straw mattress (though they usually had to share the mattress with up to a dozen other pilgrims!).

Whether one was a nobleperson, traveling with a retinue of servants or a serf, freed at the end of life to make the journey, a pilgrimage was a once-in-a-lifetime experience—oftentimes the last-of-a-lifetime. Thousands died along the pilgrimage routes; one German bishop lost almost half of his 7,000 copilgrims on a trip he organized, and the Crusades began in part because a group of 12,000 Germans was attacked by Bedouins after they left Caesarea in 1065.

Life in the Middle Ages has been famously described as "nasty, dull, brutish, and short." A pilgrimage to a far-off land was an exotic adventure to a person who might otherwise never journey more than 50 kilometers from home. In our world of easy travel, it's difficult to imagine both the trials of the pilgrim's journey and the exultation at reaching the holy shrine.

I imagine two things about ancient and medieval Christian pilgrims as compared to my pilgrimage to Taizé: I'll bet they were both more and less lonely than I am. Having now passed a week since leaving home, compounded by a country where few speak my language, a rainy and cold day, and no one here being all that welcoming, I've hit the wall. It's nowhere near the loneliness I felt while traveling in Europe in 1990, but it's still not a good feeling.

Which leads me back to the difference between me and medievals. When a person in the Middle Ages set off on a pilgrimage, it took months or even years. For me it took hours/days. For them it was on foot—some, like St. Ignatius, walked barefoot to Jerusalem. For me, today was a combination of planes, trains, and buses—my bag flew out of the bus' luggage bay on a round-about. I'm not kidding.

For them, the whole village would have come to see them off, given them money and food for the journey, and prayed for them with constancy. For me, my family drove me to the airport.

But the biggest difference must be that pilgrims in the Middle Ages were conspicuous. They wore cloaks with patches of saints on them, and they carried a special staff that denoted their pilgrimage. For those reasons, people on the way took them in and gave them food, shelter, and money. In return, the pilgrims would offer to pray for those who helped them and offer special prayers on their behalf after arriving at the holy site.

While the people I have met with know I'm on a pilgrimage, the old lady who owned the seedy hotel I stayed in Paris didn't. Neither did the nice young man who ran the hotel in London—he told me to be sure and go to the Moulin Rouge while I was in Paris. And the bus driver showed me no special grace when my bag rolled out of the bus.

Pilgrimages aren't nearly as costly (finances, time, health, death) as they used to be, but with their ease, we've lost something, too.

THEOLOGY

Abram, Moses, Jesus, and Paul traveled as a response to God's leading. But, as Paul and Peter make clear in several places, all Christians are "resident aliens." [e.g., 1 Peter 2:11] We are citizens of heaven, put on earth to "run the race to completion." [1 Corinthians 9:24 NRSV] This side of Eden, we're all wandering, trying to find our way back to that perfect place where our relationship with God is perfectly intimate. Some have sought to live out this symbolic reality: the early Irish monks wandered because they considered it a way to follow Jesus' example, much like the 18th-century Russian we met in the chapter on the Jesus Prayer.

But again, pilgrimage isn't aimless wandering. Pilgrimage has a purpose and a goal. Pilgrimage has a destination. Primeval religions before Christianity, Judaism included, held certain spots to be sacred, and the believer was blessed to be in proximity to that sacredness; "the underlying notion was that the sacred consecrates its immediate environment: hence the need to share the environment, the need for an unmediated contact with the sacred." [Melczer 2] The Lord's Table holds this kind of allure for Christians, as does a pilgrimage to the relics of a saint. And just as we touch and taste the bread and wine at the Lord's Supper, a pilgrim endeavors to make physical contact with the remains of a holy person, or with a piece of the cross or a piece of the manger.

Not surprisingly, Christians in the Middle Ages were more open to the supernatural than we are today. Stories abound about miraculous healings that resulted from contact with a relic, for these bones, like the saint whose they were, were believed to have special powers. While we might think this a holdover from pre-Christian pagan superstition, it was a doctrine officially sanctioned by the church. And when the person in need of healing was unable to make the journey, a family member could make it vicariously for her.

Another reason to make a pilgrimage was for forgiveness of sin, the arduous journey serving as penance either for one big sin or for a lifetime of iniquity. Others made the journey to fulfill a vow made at the time of ordination or in a moment of mortal danger—"Lord, if you get me out of this, I'll go to Santiago!"

And the more holy the saint, the more powerful was the shrine. Obviously, being the site of Jesus' Passion, Jerusalem was preeminent. Rome held the remains of Peter and Paul, but it took second place. James, being in the "inner circle" of disciples with Peter and John, made Santiago third. And the list went on from there.

But even if the theology of relics seems dubious today, another reason exists to make a pilgrimage: the journey itself. The medieval pilgrim was walking (at some predetermined places, crawling) for between six months and three years. Without the benefit of a Discman or an MP3 player, there was little to do but talk to your copilgrims, think, or pray. This "peripatetic meditation" had a purifying effect on the pilgrim, and pilgrims returned to their home villages changed. Not only could they tell stories of adventures and ornate cathedrals, they had been reflecting on the state of their lives for weeks on end. This kind of time alone cannot but influence how a person lives out his days.

Robert Brancatelli has written *Pilgrimage as Rite of Passage: A Guidebook for Youth Ministry*. After studying pilgrimage and taking dozens of 14-to-18 year olds on pilgrimages, he sees three steps in the journey. The first is *separation*, the time of leaving home and that which is comfortable and familiar. The next stage is the *liminal* period, when the young pilgrim is at the edge, the border, the frontier of spirituality—this is when the young person leaves her parents' faith behind and makes Christ her own. Finally, *reintegration* into the community takes place, but the former youth is now, in many ways, an adult with an individuated faith of his own.

Brancatelli points to the story of the Prodigal Son in Luke 15:11-32 as an example of this journey. The son separates (v. 11-16), experiences liminality (v. 17-20a), and is ultimately reintegrated into his family (v. 20b-24). "Pilgrimage has the potential to foster conversion in an unprecedented way," writes Brancatelli, "because it allows youth to enter the faith journey on their own terms (physically, emotionally, communally, ideologically)." [Brancatelli 55]

PRACTICE

Of course, there are all sorts of ways to make a pilgrimage, and all sorts of ways to define pilgrimage. I consider it a pilgrimage to drive the two hours to our family's cabin in Minnesota's north woods, because I consider the cabin my spiritual home. I also considered it a pilgrimage to fly across the Atlantic and visit Taizé and the Reading Boiler Room. I've also made pilgrimages to the Pine Ridge Indian Reservation in South Dakota and Assisi, Italy, two other places that are spiritually significant to me.

The point is, mental and spiritual preparation and intention are necessary for a pilgrimage to be a pilgrimage. Part of the preparation, especially for American Protestants, will be to theologically justify the idea of a pilgrimage. While mission trips to far-off lands are readily accepted by our congregations, a pilgrimage to Jerusalem, Rome, or somewhere else foreign may seem an indulgent waste of money. But while mission trips are wonderful in their own right, pilgrimages serve a different purpose, and they should be planned as such—mission trips, though they shape us inwardly, are primarily about serving others; pilgrimages are an outward expression of our own inward journeys.

No doubt, pilgrimages are physically easier now than they have ever been, but that needn't necessarily be the case. A pilgrim could, as part of the preparation, forego some of the comforts of modern travel and choose to prolong the journey by walking or riding a bike. In any case, the pilgrim should stay conscious of the purpose of the journey while on the journey. Leaving at home the Discman and *Sports Illustrated* magazine is a first step. Instead, one might take along *The Pilgrim's Progress,* John Bunyan's 17th-century masterpiece allegory of a Christian's journey from the "City of Destruction" to the "Heavenly City."

Choosing the destination is, obviously, of great importance. Each denomination within the Christian tradition has its own natural pilgrimages. Beyond that, any Christian may become enamored of a certain saint's writings and desire to walk in that person's footsteps. St. Francis of Assisi has had a profound influence on many within the church, and his aura still permeates his hometown in the Umbrian hills of Italy. The Christian community of Northumbria in England has attracted pilgrims recently because of its commitment to communal living and worship. Those who love the writing of Francis Schaefer head to L'Abri; others follow the music to Taizé; Lutherans might head to Wittenberg,

The journey home, too, is a pilgrimage of sorts. Bus, train, bus, plane, plane—that's the order this time. I've determined to tell my fellow travelers the type of journey I'm on this time, and let them think what they will. Reactions vary, but most people are interested.

On the ninth day of sabbatical, I'm really falling in love with praying the Daily Office, particularly the prayers said before bed at Compline. To pray for all those "who watch, work, and weep this night...for the sick...for the dying...for the grieving." Those prayers really serve to put life in perspective, especially at the end of what I would consider a long and grueling day, but I am reminded every night before I fall asleep that the hospitals are all full, that parents, spouses, children, and friends all grieve somewhere, and that others have needs that are far more poignant than mine.

Episcopalians to Canterbury. The pilgrimage will gain meaning in the importance of the destination to the pilgrim.

And, of course, the more time that can be taken for the journey, the more impact the trip is likely to have. A weekend sojourn isn't likely to affect the pilgrim as much as a three-month sabbatical pilgrimage to a foreign land. Not everyone can make the time for an extended trip, but the bottom line is, the longer the better. (That is, to a certain point; in the Middle Ages, pilgrimages were sometimes abused when people used them to escape their duties at home.) Indeed, the best pilgrimages may be years in the planning and months in the making. In fact, now might be the time to make a vow to God for a pilgrimage upon your retirement.

THOUGHTS FOR YOUTH MINISTRY

As Robert Brancatelli points out in *Pilgrimage as Rite of Passage*, something powerful happens when adolescents are taken on a pilgrimage:

Pilgrimage works catechetically by providing opportunities for youth to experience conversion in a context that makes sense to them (in their own language, stories, music, relationships). It does this while providing movement, identity, and ritual expression. Pilgrims build community among themselves while on the journey and, if the journey is extended, while spending days and nights together. During this time they share stories and learn about their faith through the study of Scripture, church history or the pilgrimage site itself. Gradually, the church becomes integrated into the developing relationships and witnessing that occur among pilgrims en route to the site. These faith stories weave their way into the emerging identity of youth. [Brancatelli 53]

This comes as no surprise to those of us engaged in youth work—much of our best ministry takes place on retreats, camps, adventure trips, and mission trips. Travel has been a cornerstone of most youth ministries for years. If youth workers have made a mistake, it's been not taking the *travel* itself seriously enough. For the journey itself can be transformed into a sacred journey with some thought and some theological reflection by the leader and the students. As the leaders of the thousands of trips that American youth groups take every year, we have the opportunity to shape these into experiences of pilgrimage. Put a copy of *The Pilgrim's Progress* into your students' hands to read on a trip; schedule stops along the way at noteworthy churches; facilitate discussions in the van about the "journey of life with God."

As a part of Confirmation or discipleship programs, many churches take students on pilgrimages to a sites important in their traditions. Catholics attend World Youth Day, an official pilgrimage in their tradition; they also visit Lourdes, Fatima, and Guadalupe. Methodists visit Aldersgate, the spot where John Wesley felt his heart "strangely warmed." Presbyterian and Reformed Christians can visit Geneva and see the pulpit from which John Calvin preached his many influential sermons. Congregationalists go to New England to visit the sites made famous by their Pilgrim forebears. Baptists can visit the temple in London where Charles Spurgeon held forth three times per week to massive crowds. Episcopalians and Anglicans follow Chaucer's merry band to Canterbury Cathedral. Lutherans stand before the door in Wittenberg on which Martin Luther posted the Ninety-Five Theses. Orthodox Christians travel to Istanbul (formerly Constantinople) to be overwhelmed by the grandeur of the Hagia Sophia.

Each of these spots brings to life part of the story of the Christian church that specifically relates to each denomination. The learning becomes concrete and experiential as a 15-year-old Lutheran stands, looking at the door in Wittenberg, and hearing how courageous Luther was for speaking out about the church's abuses. I hardly need to argue that this learning experience will last a lifetime, while reading about Luther in a book or hearing about him from a pastor back home most likely won't.

Deliberate intention, again, is the key to success. Think through your summer trips for next year. Does one of them lend itself to being shaped as a pilgrimage? Can you fit a true pilgrimage into your summer plans over the next couple of years? Take Brancatelli's advice and make pilgrimage a rite of passage in your ministry.

A FINAL WORD

Book V of the *Codex Calixtinus*, the medieval guide for pilgrims to Santiago, gives advice to those who meet pilgrims along the way—advice we can all heed:

Pilgrims, whether poor or rich, who return from or proceed to Santiago, must be received charitably and respectfully by all. For he who welcomes them and provides them diligently with lodging will have as his guest not merely the Blessed James, but the Lord himself, who in his gospels said: "He who welcomes you, welcomes me." Many are those who in the past brought upon themselves the wrath of God because they refused to receive the pilgrims of Saint James or the indigent. [Melczer 132]

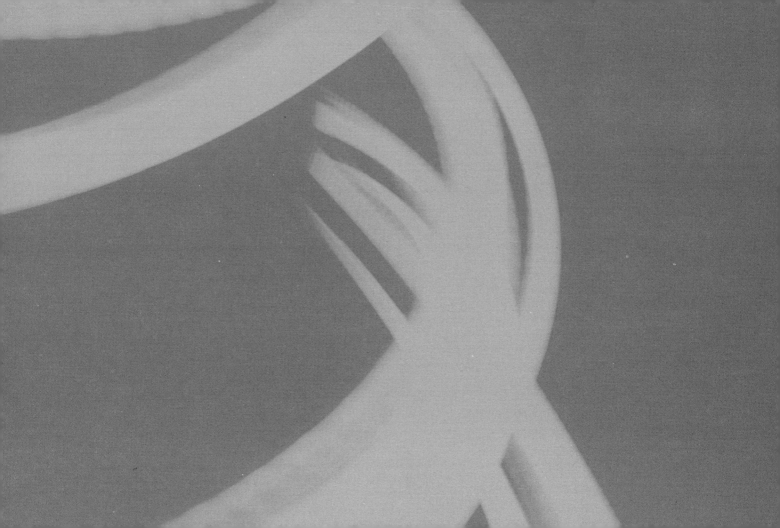

Chapter 15
Fasting

Arm yourself manfully against the wickedness of the devil; control the appetite, and you will more easily control all bodily desires.

Thomas à Kempis

Lilly Lewin, a youth worker in Ohio, tells this story:

In August of 2001, we were getting ready to begin a new worship service specifically designed for students. Being a very liturgical "High" Episcopal church, founded in the 1860s, we had our work cut out for us. Miraculously, the Vestry (board) had approved major money for technology (laptop, PowerPoint® projector, sound system, etc.), and enough to really get stuff off the ground. So it was time for the vision to become reality.

We were going to build the plane as we flew it—not always the best plan, but around the Episcopal church we can talk an idea to death before ever attempting anything! I'm the kind of person who likes to jump in with both feet! (You can always ask for a towel!)

So we (the royal we…meaning I) decided to follow the lead of Dan Slatter of Warehouse in Chichester, England, and design a Forty Day Stand: 40 days of prayer and fasting centered around a prayer journal (focused on our new service), a weekly day of fasting (Tuesdays), and the breaking of the fast together on Tuesday nights. We would meet on Tuesday nights to eat together, pray and plan for the new worship service.

We counted back from our start date (September 16) and began in early August. We (all of our leaders, which numbered five) challenged ourselves and our students to fast.

For most of us it was our first attempt at a day of fasting from food—in Episcopal Land we do tend to give up stuff for Lent, but this had a different feel and purpose. This was our community of kids coming together to build something with God. I admit, I am the world's worst faster; I have never been good at fasting, and until the Forty Day Stand, even my juice fasts had flopped! I always ended up eating!

But this fast wasn't just about food. The food fast was planned for Tuesdays—not eating after dinner Monday night and eating again at our prayer and planning meeting Tuesday night. We challenged our students to fast from other things besides food, like Nintendo, Play Station, shopping, and TV.

One seventh grader admitted that he gave up Nintendo for a week, but he really didn't like it or feel like he got anything out of the process.

Being a televisionaholic, I chose to fast from TV for the 40 days. I discovered just how much I used TV as a filler, as background when I walked into a room. And I realized just what a time-stealer TV can be. It was a powerful realization.

For me, not eating on Tuesdays became easier as the weeks went by. Having purpose for the fast and having the community support and incentive fueled my ability to pray rather than eat.

Getting together as a group to break the fast was key! We really built camaraderie waiting for the pizza to arrive on Tuesday nights—everyone was ready to EAT! Then we were ready to brainstorm, pray, and plan the service. The students prayed for new folks to come and friends to invite. They also got to say just what they wanted and didn't want in a worship service ("Nothing like Sunday morning!" was a familiar quote). After brainstorming a short list of names and praying over them for a week, the "new thing" became OASIS! OASIS Sacred Space kicked off a couple weeks later. We had prayed for 40 people, and guess what? Forty folks filled our worship space! God is really amazing! We just should have prayed for more!

P.S. Oh yeah, by the way, our prayers for a worship band didn't get answered. Instead we learned that worship is what we do with God 24/7 and not just 20 minutes of singing at the beginning of a service.

Lilly added this: Rory is an eighth grade boy. He's totally athletic, plays baseball, basketball, and football and really loves to skateboard. *And* he was my best 'evangelist' last year for OASIS. He would always bring two or three friends with him—all preppy skateboarders, many who didn't go anywhere else to church. Several of these guys became regulars at our Sacred Space services. They'd skateboard for an hour, eat pizza, and then participate in Sacred Space. These are Rory's thoughts on the Forty Day Stand we did last summer. He was just getting ready to start seventh grade!

"Last summer I gave up breakfast for the entire 40 days. It was hard at first 'cause I got pretty hungry. But after a while, it got easier and I got used to not having breakfast. I'd gotten used to 11 years straight of having breakfast. There were days when I really wanted to eat, but I didn't. It made me think about things going on and about the good things in my life. I also read the Bible a few times when I really wanted to eat and it (the Bible) wasn't as boring as it use to be. It was the first time I ever fasted. It was harder than it seemed…hard not to break it. But I could do it again. It was good. It made me realize what it feels like to feel full."

HISTORY

Fasting is a practice common to most religions, both major and minor. It's seen as a sacrifice that gains favor with the divine, demonstrates self-control, and purifies the body. In the Old Testament, there are both public and private fasts, each for different reasons. Public fasts were proclaimed by prophets and monarchs as a sign of national mourning. They were always accompanied by prayer, and often by the wearing of sackcloth and ashes as a sign of penance for sins.

Occasionally, public fasts were called at an inauspicious time, like the four days of fasting declared after the fall of Jerusalem, and observed for 70 years. [Zechariah 7:5, 8:19] In the midst of a lengthy screed, calling Israel back to God, the prophet Joel cries, "Declare a holy fast; call a sacred assembly. Summon the elders and all who live in the land to the house of the Lord your God, and cry out to the Lord." [Joel 1:14]

Other public fasts were normative and connected to holy days. *Yom Kippur*, the Day of Atonement, was the one annual fast day proscribed for the entirety of Israel's existence:

This is to be a lasting ordinance for you: On the tenth day of the seventh month you must deny yourselves and not do any work—whether native-born or an alien living among you—because on this day atonement will be made for you, to cleanse you. Then, before the Lord , you will be clean from all your sins. It is a sabbath of rest, and you must deny yourselves; it is a lasting ordinance. [Leviticus 16:29-31]

Here "deny yourselves" means to fast from all food and drink, as well as other bodily gratifications. These annual fasts were followed by feasts, celebrating the Lord's goodness in granting forgiveness to the people.

Private fasts were held for similar reasons. The psalmist says he fasted because others whom he loved had become ill, [Psalm 35:13-14] and when scorned, he fasted until his knees were weak. [Psalm 109: 24] But, like public fasts, most individual fasts were done for the sake of penance for sin, as when David fasted over the fate of his infant child, born to Bathsheba. [2 Samuel 12:15-23]

In the New Testament, John the Baptist's followers were known for their fasting, and Jesus continued the biblical exhortations for fasting, both in his teaching ("But when you fast, put oil on your head and wash your face, so that it will not be obvious to men that you are fasting, but only to your Father, who is unseen; and your Father, who sees what is done in secret, will reward you" [Matthew 6:17-18]) and in his example ("Then Jesus was led by the Spirit into the desert to be tempted by the devil. After fasting forty days and forty nights, he was hungry." [Matthew 4:1-2]).

In the early church, the Apostles were known to fast regularly, and by the time the *Didache* was written around A.D. 60, Christians were observing every Wednesday and Friday as fast days. Just as *Yom Kippur* was an annual fast of repentance for the Jews, Christians observed a repentance fast in the days leading up to Easter. Although it started as only two days, by the fourth century it had expanded to the 40 days we now know as Lent. In the East, three more periods of fasting were added, including Advent (the four weeks preceding Christmas), the Fast of the Apostles in June, and the Fast of the Theotokos (Virgin Mary) in August.

Ancient Christians often followed strict fasting guidelines, abstaining from all food on fast days. Others refrained from meat, eggs, butter, and cheese—these are still the requirements for many Orthodox Christians. Roman Catholics observe only Ash Wednesday and Good Friday as official fast days; during the rest of Lent they are to take only one large meal at midday and a small meal in the evening. Protestants have generally not emphasized fasting, even though Luther, Wesley, and Calvin all commended the practice. Recently, as Protestants have recovered the rhythms of the liturgical year, fasting during Lent has become more common.

THEOLOGY

"The Christian fast signifies, above all, an exercise of penitence and sacrifice; but, already for the Fathers, it also had the aim of rendering man more open to the encounter with God and making a Christian more capable of self-dominion and at the same time more attentive to those in need." [www.vatican.va] Indeed, fasting is univocally commended by the Fathers of the early church—along with its partners prayer and silence, it's the universally applied spiritual discipline:

Abba John the Dwarf: "If a king wanted to take possession of his enemies' city, he would begin by cutting off the water and the food and so his enemies, dying of hunger, would submit to him. It is the same with the passions of the flesh: if a man goes about fasting and hungry, the enemies of his soul grow weak." [Ward 74]

"Abba Joseph asked Abba Poemen, 'How should one fast?' Abba Poemen said to him, 'For my part, I think it is better that one should eat every day, but only a little, so as not to be satisfied." [Ward 144]

Amma Syncletica: "Just as the most bitter medicine drives out poisonous creatures so prayer joined to fasting drives evil thoughts away." [Ward 193]

Abba Hyperechios: "Fasting is a check against sin for the monk. He who discards it is like a rampaging stallion." [Ward 200]

St. Gregory of Sinai: "There are three levels of partaking of food: abstinence, adequacy, and satiety. To abstain means to remain a little hungry after eating; to eat adequately means neither to be hungry nor to be weighed down; to be satiated means to be slightly weighed down. But eating beyond satiety is the door to belly-madness, through which lust comes in. But you, firm in this knowledge, choose what is best for you, according to your powers, without overstepping the limits." [Kadloubovsky 79-80]

St. Benedict: "We believe that two cooked dishes will satisfy the daily needs at each meal—at the sixth and ninth hours…two dishes must be enough for all…. Nothing is more contrary to being a Christian than gluttony." [Meisel 80]

We could go on and on; the saints of the church speak with one voice: gluttony is a great sin and fasting is a great virtue. The reason: fasting aids in that great Christian quality, the "mortification of the flesh." Since earliest time—indeed it's a concept set forth powerfully by Jesus and Paul—the appetites or lusts of the body are seen as the root of much evil. Of course, any human being can appreciate the inner battle between the good that the "spirit" wants and the sin that is the tendency of our "flesh."

I use quotation marks around those two, because they are separated by a false dichotomy. Neither the Hebrew worldview nor Jesus recognized the body-spirit duality that was made famous by Plato and Augustine. In fact, the "mortal coil" which is our physical body is unified with our soul/spirit, and, instead of weakening a theology of fasting, this holistic interpretation strengthens it. Physical disciplines aid our spiritual development precisely *because* the body and the soul are so intricately intertwined.

Thus, one reason we fast is to develop self-control. No concept of personal and corporate spirituality is more central to the Pauline writings than the ideal of self-control. Whether it's with food, sex, words, or even church government, Paul consistently urges moderation and self-control: "Everyone who competes in the games goes into strict training. They do it to get a crown that will not last; but we do it to get a crown that will last forever. Therefore I do not run like a man running aimlessly; I do not fight like a man beating the air. No, I beat my body and make it my slave so that after I have preached to others, I myself will not be disqualified for the prize." [1 Corinthians 9:25-27]

And in a world like ours where, unlike the saints quoted previously, food is known in an unparalleled abundance, fasting is an even more worthy discipline. Two paragraphs from Marjorie Thompson's book, *Soul Feast*, articulate this so clearly that they bear repeating in full:

In a more tangible, visceral way than any other spiritual discipline, fasting reveals our excessive attachments and the assumptions that lie behind them. Food is necessary to life, but we have made it more necessary than God. How often have we neglected to remember God's presence when we would never consider neglecting to eat! Fasting brings us face to face with how we put the material world ahead of its spiritual source....

Perhaps we can see, then, that the discipline of fasting has to do with the critical dynamic of *accepting those limits which are life-restoring*. Our culture would seduce us into believing that we can have it all, do it all, and (even more preposterous!) that we deserve it all. Yet in refusing to accept limits on our consumption or activity, we perpetuate a death-dealing dynamic in the world. That is why the discipline of fasting is so profoundly important today. [Thompson 71, 74]

PRACTICE

Exhibiting self-control and abiding by self-imposed limits are antithetical to our consumer-driven culture. The Desert Fathers and Mothers found it so difficult to maintain a life of prayer, silence, and fasting in Jerusalem and other cities that they retreated to the wilderness—and they had never seen a billboard or a TV ad! There can be no denying that we live in a world that promotes gluttony and consumption. And the almost weekly news stories and medical reports on "America's Expanding Waistline" corroborate our weakness in this area.

Fasting is a spiritual remedy to what is, really, a spiritual problem. To fast shows our reliance upon God for all things. It reminds us that we are, ultimately, spiritual beings. It confirms that "man does not live by bread alone"; "Everyone who drinks of this water will be thirsty again, but those who drink of the water that I will give them will never be thirsty"; "This is my body which is broken for you"; and "I am the bread of life."

In the end, fasting trains us in righteousness and as we practice this form of self-control, we are not in it alone—because, of course, Paul rounds out his list of the fruit of the Spirit in the letter to the Galatians with self-control. [Galatians 5:22-23]

Fasting from food and drink is the type of fast indicated in Scripture. Richard Foster delineates three types of fasts in *Celebration of Discipline*. A "normal fast" is to abstain from all food and drink except water. A "partial fast" is to limit the food intake to significantly less than normal. And an "absolute fast" is to refrain from any eating or drinking. [Foster 49] Fasting is known to have health benefits when done correctly, but a spiritual fast obviously has different motivations. Even so, fasting should be done carefully and, if possible, under the guidance of a physician.

Most individuals find fasting exceedingly difficult because food has both a physical and psychological hold on us. When fasting, one should also moderate one's level of activity—working out, traveling, or not getting enough sleep can lead to sickness or more serious health problems. My experience has been that weakness and muscle soreness is particularly acute upon missing the first and second meals. Beyond that, the feelings of hunger tend to abate somewhat, giving way to spiritual clarity.

But the psychological dependence on food can be even harder to break. Like the college frat boy who feels naked without a beer in his hand at a party, most of us pattern our lives around three meals and many snacks per day, and we feel incomplete without the oral fixation of food (or coffee or chewing gum…). One of the disciplines of the fast is to find other prayerful or otherwise productive ways to use the time usually spent eating and drinking.

For the novice, fasting should be practiced gradually at the beginning. In the week before a fast, smaller meals should be eaten to allow the stomach to shrink. It's beneficial to try several partial fasts before attempting a normal fast. And because the risk of dehydration is high even in a normal fast (we get much of our water in food, so someone on a normal fast should drink lots of water), an absolute fast should be attempted only by someone experienced in fasting who is called to it by God.

There are other fasts, too. As Lilly mentions at the opening of this chapter, it can be a powerful practice to participate in either a personal or a communal fast from television. Julie and I fasted from TV several times until we decided that we would watch no TV every year between Memorial Day and Labor Day. We've also committed ourselves to never having more than one TV in our house. You can imagine the extra time we have to do things like talk, take walks, and write books! Other things to fast from might be trashy magazines, gossip, video games, makeup, or shopping. As with food, any of these can have a stranglehold on our spiritual lives—a stranglehold that can be broken with a fast.

THOUGHTS FOR YOUTH MINISTRY

On the last weekend in February, most of the students in our ministry fast from noon on Friday until 6 p.m. on Saturday as part of World Vision's 30-Hour Famine. The kids get sponsors, and every year tens of thousands of dollars are raised for hunger relief and development work in Peru. But it also gives us a chance to participate in an annual public fast. The fact that over half a million kids around the globe are fasting on the same days adds to the communal feel. But, as well as raising money, we also use the fasting experience as a time to emphasize one of the biblical themes of fasting. One year it might be fasting for personal and corporate repentance, another year for forgiveness and reconciliation, another year to stand in solidarity with the hungry, and another to focus on those who are ill.

The Famine has consistently been one of the most spiritually powerful times of the year. Last year Emily, an eighth grader, wrote this poem during the Famine:

Hunger is difficult to describe.

It turns on and off time.

(What I mean by that is when hunger is

Affecting you the time passes slowly.)

You may feel an emptiness or

Your stomach may just growl.

You may not feel it even though it always

Seems to be there.

Or maybe it's all you can think about

And your mind just doesn't seem to be there.

It is difficult to imagine that some

People deal with it every day.

There's no telling what to say.

I can go back and eat, it was my choice

To starve.

But what happens when the only

Food you've ever known is sloppy

Mush?

Fasting with middle and high school students has its own set of challenges. We encourage the students to drink 100 percent fruit juice so that they are staying hydrated and getting some calories during the 30 hours. We also have to answer lots of parents' questions about the safety of fasting for youth, including some concerns about eating disorders. Physicians have told me that while fasting can sometimes be used to mask eating disorders, it's not known to cause them. Of course, some students with health concerns like diabetes are unable to fast, but they can still participate in the weekend's activities and eat unobtrusively.

Lent, being the universal Christian fast, is a great time to introduce fasting to the students. You might make a group pact to eat half the lunch you normally would or skip a meal every Friday. In the book, *Way to Live: Christian Practices for Teens*, high school sophomore Alexx Campbell gave away one material possession each of the 40 days of Lent—he found it both challenging and rewarding. In any case, remember that even during Lent, Sundays are always feast days!

A FINAL WORD

John Chrysostom, the greatest theologian in the Eastern tradition, preached this:

Dost thou fast? Give me proof of it by thy works!

Is it said by what kind of works?

If thou seest a poor man, take pity on him!

If thou seest an enemy, be reconciled to him!

If thou seest a friend gaining honor, envy him not!

If thou seest a handsome woman, pass her by!

For let not the mouth only fast, but also the eye, and ear, and the feet, and the hands, and all the members of our bodies.

Let the hands fast, by being pure from rapine and avarice.

Let the feet fast, by ceasing from running to the unlawful spectacles.

Let the eyes fast, being taught never to fix themselves rudely upon handsome countenances, or to busy themselves with strange beauties.

For looking is the food of the eyes, but if this be such as is unlawful or forbidden, it mars the fast; and upsets the whole safety of the soul; but if it be lawful and safe, it adorns fasting.

For it would be among things the most absurd to abstain from lawful food because of the fast, but with the eyes to touch even what is forbidden. Dost thou not eat flesh? Feed not upon lasciviousness by means of the eyes.

Let the ear fast also. The fasting of the ear consists in refusing to receive evil speakings and calumnies. "Thou shalt not receive a false report," it says. [www.ccel.org]

Mary Emily Briehl Wells, a high school senior, wrote this about public fasting in *Way to Live*:

Sometimes Christians fast, refraining from certain or all food and drink for a day or a season…. Fasting is a way to say yes to life, together. Ancient communities conserved food during the winter when animals were hibernating and fields lay barren. They restricted their eating so that they could all live until the next harvest. Then they feasted! For Christians, too, fasting is not primarily a solitary discipline any more than feasting is a private event. We fast with others: our Bible study or youth group, our family or congregation. Fasting with others helps focus our attention on the community and God rather than ourselves. [Bass (2002) 73]

Chapter 16

The Sign of the Cross and Other Bodily Prayers

If you confide in the Lord, strength will be given you from heaven, and the world and the flesh shall be made subject to you. Neither will you fear your enemy, the devil, if you be armed with faith and signed with the cross of Christ.

Thomas à Kempis

Jay Folley is a youth worker at the Church of Saint Patrick in Edina, Minnesota, and he's a great friend to me. He wrote this:

Every morning there is that heroic moment in which I need to decide between popping out of bed and hitting the snooze button (in which case, the opportunity will arise again and again every 10 minutes or so). Over the years I have fallen into the habit of signing myself with the cross as an intentional way of beginning my day. And I am careful that I sincerely mean to begin the day at that point and not in fact go back to sleep. Because if I decide to reach for my forehead and not the snooze button, the game is on, the day is consecrated to God and I mean to make the most of it.

As I make the sign of the cross, I pray: "God come to my assistance. Lord make haste to help me. Glory be to the Father, and the Son, and the Holy Spirit, as it was in the beginning, is now, and will be forever. Amen."

When I first began this practice, I waited until my feet hit the floor in order to pray; in fact, sometimes I would fall to my knees next to my bed. I loved the very deliberateness of the act, the physical acknowledgment that I need God in order to get through this day. Now however, more often than not, I lie in bed and pray. It may seem that I have gotten lazier, and perhaps I have (to say that I am not a morning person is an understatement), but the intention remains, and in fact, my morning offerings have grown longer and more meaningful. As I lie in the warmth of my bed praying and asking God that I might live according to his will this day, it seems to me more appropriate to be comfortable and secure, as a child would in his father's arms.

This is important to realize: we are body and soul, physical and spiritual, and the prayer and the posture impact each other in profound ways.

There are times when I walk into the chapel at St. Pat's and sit cross-legged at the feet of our Lord. Other times I feel I should kneel, and occasionally I will lie face down. Sometimes as I am sitting in the pew I find myself relaxed, palms open, indicating receptivity, other times I find my head buried in my hands or chest and I feel like I am searching inwardly.

Your body can tell you a lot about how you are praying. Just recently a student walked into the chapel as I was preparing for a talk and caught me pacing up and down the center aisle. I

HISTORY

realized that I had come to the chapel for peace and inspiration, but had not disposed myself to receive either.

Here then is the secret to all of this—the sign of the cross, kneeling, genuflecting, praying with your hands in the air—these things are not formulas or magic. They do not in themselves produce grace. They are as efficacious as the person is open to receiving the gifts of God. A quick, mindless sign of the cross is as worthless as the Lord's Prayer said in boredom. But a humble and contrite heart coupled with prostrating yourself at the feet of Jesus…oh my…I can only recommend that you try it. It will touch you—body and soul.

While Adam, Abraham, and Moses had the distinct pleasure of conversing with God—Exodus 33:11 states that "The Lord would speak to Moses face to face, as a man speaks with his friend"—more recent followers of God have often felt compelled to use bodily gestures when speaking to the Creator. Biblical prayer postures will be described briefly below in the Theology section, but instead of trying to track the history of multiple gestures, let's look exclusively at one.

The "sign of the cross" is known mostly as a Catholic and Orthodox practice, having fallen into disrepute among the Reformers for being superstitious. However, this gesture has a long and rich history in the church. Here is a sampling of what some Early Church Fathers wrote about this type of prayer:

Tertullian (c.160-c.225): "In all our travels and movement, in all our coming in and going out, in putting on of our shoes, at the bath, at the table, in lighting our candles, in lying down, in sitting down, whatever employment occupies us, we mark our foreheads with the sign of the cross."

Hippolytus (c.170-c.236): "When tempted, always reverently seal your forehead with the sign of the cross. For this sign of the Passion is displayed and made manifest against the devil if you make it in faith, not in order that you may be seen by men, but by your knowledge putting it forward like a shield."

Cyril of Jerusalem (c.315-387): "Let us then not be ashamed to confess the Crucified. Be the cross our seal, made with boldness by our fingers on our brow and in every thing; over the bread we eat and the cups we drink, in our comings and in goings; before our sleep, when we lie down and when we awake; when we are traveling, and when we are at rest." [www.scbor-romeo.org]

Early Christians marked themselves with the sign of the cross in several ways: one was to use the thumb to make a small cross on the forehead, the lips, and the chest, thereby asking that God would bless everything thought, spoken, and felt in the heart. Everything in the day was sanctified by this sign, and temptations and evil were thwarted as well. Some evidence exists that Christians also used this sign surreptitiously to identify one another during times of persecution.

By the middle of the first millennium A.D., Christianity was well known and public throughout the Roman Empire. The sign of the cross developed into a more bold profession, with the right hand touching first the forehead, then the chest, then the right and left shoulders. At some point during the Middle Ages, the Western rite of the Roman Catholic church changed to left shoulder-right shoulder, while Byzantine Catholics and Orthodox Christians still make the sign with the right shoulder first.

The position of the fingers also has changed over the years. At first, the small and stealthy sign was made on the forehead using the thumb. The Monophysite controversy of the fifth and sixth centuries introduced a change. The controversy was over the true nature of Jesus Christ: Monophysites argued that Christ had one true nature, but the Council of Chalcedon (451) established that Jesus Christ was one person with two natures (human and divine). In order to physically display their orthodoxy, Christians began to make the sign of the cross with two fingers held together, the index and middle fingers, symbolizing the two natures.

Later, a tradition developed in the East that also influenced the West in which the thumb was held together with the slightly bent index and middle fingers to represent the Trinity and the ring and pinky fingers were bent all the way to the palm to represent the two natures of Christ. While that form is still practiced in the East, Western Christians make the sign of the cross either with the tips of all five fingers held together, representing the five wounds of Christ, or with the thumb over the bent index finger, forming a cross. In fact, some Roman Catholics kiss their thumb as a sign of reverence to the cross in this lattermost form.

Different verbal prayers have accompanied the sign of the cross over the years. Some of these are:

"The sign of Christ"

"The seal of the living God"

"In the name of Jesus"

"In the name of Jesus of Nazareth"

"In the name of the Holy Trinity"

"Our help is in the name of the Lord"

"O God come to my assistance; O Lord make haste to help me"

"In the name of the Father and of the Son and of the Holy Ghost" (currently used in the West)

"Holy God, Holy strong One, Holy Immortal One, Have mercy on us" (currently used in the East). [www.newadvent.org]

So we see, as this practice of prayer has developed over the centuries, it has taken on new meaning and new richness, with even the position of the fingers carrying theological implications. Far from being superstitious, it's a way to engage our bodies in our otherwise too-often cerebral prayers. The *Catechism of the Catholic Church* says of this practice:

"The sign of the cross…marks with the imprint of Christ the one who is going to belong to him and signifies the grace of the redemption Christ won for us by his cross." [CCC, section 1235]

"The Christian begins his day, his prayers, and his activities with the sign of the cross: 'In the name of the Father and of the Son and of the Holy Spirit. Amen.' The baptized person dedicates the day to the glory of God and calls on the Savior's grace which lets him act in the spirit as a child of the Father. The sign of the cross strengthens us in temptations and difficulties." [CCC, section 2157]

THEOLOGY

Other physical gestures and postures have been used by people at prayer since biblical times, each one carrying its own theological significance.

Spreading the Palms: This is the most common prayer gesture mentioned in the Bible (e.g., "Then Moses left Pharaoh and went out of the city. He spread out his hands toward the LORD; the thunder and hail stopped, and the rain no longer poured down on the land." [Exodus 9:33]). This position is one of petition, in which the pray-er is asking God to fill her hands by granting the request. In early Christian art, the *orant* (Latin, 'beg, plead, pray') was a popular depiction; it's a painting of a figure, either kneeling or standing, with arms outstretched in prayer, which can be found in the catacombs in Rome and on sarcophagi from the period.

Bending Over, Stooping, Kneeling: The one who delivers the first fruits of the harvest is called upon to bend over as an act of humility before the Lord in Deuteromony 26:10; the prophet Ezekiel commands everyone who approaches the Temple to bow; the psalmist sings, "Come, let us bow down in worship, let us kneel before the Lord our Maker; for he is our God and we are the people of his pasture, the flock under his care." [Psalm 95:6-7] All these postures are signs of reverence and humility which remind the pray-er of his subservience to God.

A common practice among Roman Catholics today is *genuflection*, in which the pray-er shows reverence for God and God's holy things by bending down on the right knee. In the Orthodox Church, the similar gesture is *mytania*, a bow from the hips, with the legs straight. In both cases, the believer signifies bodily that he is repentant, humble, and in need of God's grace, this being the spirit with which a Christian should enter worship.

Prostration: The ultimate sign of humility, to prostrate oneself is to lie face down on the ground. It was, for centuries, the homage paid by a defeated warrior to the victor in battle; the loser of a battle would lie on the ground and allow the victor to stand on his back. It is a sign of submission, helplessness, and even death. It's also the posture that several people took when they met Jesus:

While Jesus was in one of the towns, a man came along who was covered with leprosy. When he saw Jesus, he fell with his face to the ground and begged him, "Lord, if you are willing, you can make me clean." Jesus reached out his hand and touched the man. "I am willing," he said. "Be clean!" And immediately the leprosy left him. [Luke 5:12-13]

Other examples of people who fell and prostrated themselves at Jesus' feet are the Syrophoenician woman, [Mark 7:24-30] Jairus, [Mark 5:21ff.] and Legion. [Luke 8:26-38] And today, Catholic priests prostrate themselves during their ordination ceremony as a sign of their utter obedience to Christ.

Of course, Christians have prayed in every imaginable posture down through the years, some with more theological heft than others. The truth on which all these positions rest is that we human beings are body and spirit. We have ultimately one, not two natures. Although Plato and other philosophers divided the flesh from the soul, the Hebrew conception that Jesus practiced has always been that those two parts of humans are united. What we do with our bodies affects our souls, and what we do with our souls affects our bodies.

Therefore, to kneel before God in prayer, whether done privately or in a public worship setting, not only shows God we are humble before him, but it also *does something to us*. And if you really want to have your soul pierced with humility, try prostrating yourself before the Lord in worship.

PRACTICE

Kneeling has gotten a bad rap in some circles, because it's "required" in some forms of worship. However, if you talk to someone theologically trained in Catholicism, Orthodoxy, or Anglicanism, you will find that in fact it's never required. To kneel after taking the Eucharist in a Catholic mass, for instance, shows reverence for the Lord's Supper. Although many Catholics consider it obligatory, it's meant to be an individual response by the believer.

Similarly, Catholic apologist Al Kresta writes this about genuflection:

Why do Catholics genuflect?

Catholics genuflect because we are in rehearsal for that regenerating moment at the end of history "when every knee shall bow and every tongue confess that Jesus is Lord to the glory of God the Father." [Philippians 2:10-11] We're a little slow at learning, so we thought we'd begin early.

Genuflection is such a small thing. We bend the right knee to the floor and rise up again before a holy person or object. But it's a little gesture that demonstrates some big things: repentance, petition, veneration.

THOUGHTS FOR YOUTH MINISTRY

It means that Catholics believe that there is something beyond this material world that we turn to, appeal to, and honor. It means we aren't a law unto ourselves. It means we believe that there is a principle of hierarchy in the universe to which we submit.

In this simple act lies a whole view of God, man, time, eternity, sin, salvation, spirit, and matter. It is a small but submissive response to what God has done in revealing himself to us. [Kresta 11]

Any Christian would be hard pressed to disagree with the theology that underlies the act of genuflecting. But, as with any spiritual practice, when the action becomes a meaningless obligation rather than a heartfelt response, something important has been lost. The same could be said of raising hands in some Protestant circles—it has become expected as opposed to sincere. So, the key to practicing a prayer posture is authenticity of spirit.

Ultimately, each of us will find physical postures that best lead us into God's presence. For some it will be standing with hands raised, for others kneeling, and for others sitting with our hands folded or open. Some people will find great meaning in the sign of the cross, while others won't. Since none of these is biblically mandated, it's an open invitation to try them all and discover which is most meaningful for you.

Probably the best thing you can do is get your students to try praying with postures and gestures that are outside of your own tradition. If you're Catholic, encourage your students to raise their hands as they sing. If you're Pentecostal, have them try crossing themselves whenever you end a prayer in the name of the Father, Son, and Holy Spirit.

Of course, it's not appropriate to force them to do anything, but to suggest and encourage can be powerful for two reasons. First, it will open up the practice of other Christian traditions and make your students less judgmental of them—especially when you explain the theology behind a posture. And secondly, when they go back to the gestures common to your tradition, they'll be more mindful of the meanings behind them.

To visit the worship service of another tradition is most helpful in this regard. Observing, and even taking part in the kneeling and sign of the cross in a Catholic worship service, the kissing of an icon in an Orthodox service, or the ecstatic prayer with hands raised of a Charismatic service will open your students' eyes—maybe yours, too! You can meet with one of the clergy members of that church before or after the service to ask about the meanings behind the movements.

A FINAL WORD

And you can bet that some of your students will find some of these postures very meaningful. In fact, don't be surprised if they start to do them in public worship settings. I can only imagine what could happen if a bunch of our students started kneeling to pray during our traditional brand of Reformed worship—look out...a revival may be around the corner!

In his biography of the life of St. Anthony (c. 251-356), St. Athanasius (c.296-373) quotes Anthony and shows how potent early Christians considered the sign of the cross:

Neither ought we to fear the appearances of evil spirits. For they are nothing, but quickly vanish, especially if one defend himself by faith and the sign of the cross. [www.ccel.org]

Chapter 17
Sabbath

The spiritual person puts the care of his soul before all else.

Thomas à Kempis

During what turned out to be his last year of life, Henri Nouwen was granted a year-long sabbatical. At the time, he was serving as the chaplain at Daybreak, a community for the developmentally disabled in Toronto. He kept a daily journal that year which was posthumously published as *Sabbatical Journey: The Diary of His Final Year*. This is from the first entry, dated September 2, 1995:

This is the first day of my sabbatical. I am excited and anxious, hopeful and fearful, tired, and full of desire to do a thousand things. The coming year stretches out in front of me as a long, open field full of flowers and full of weeds. How will I cross that field? What will I have learned when I finally reach the other end?...

I feel strange! Very happy and very scared at the same time. I have always dreamt about a whole year without appointments, meetings, lectures, travels, letters, and phone calls, a year completely open to let something radically new happen. But can I do it? Can I let go of all the things that make me feel useful and significant? I realize that I am quite addicted to be busy and experience a bit of withdrawal anxiety. I have to nail myself to a chair and control these wild impulses to get up again and become busy with whatever draws my attention.

But underneath all these anxieties, there is an immense joy. Free at last! Free to think critically, to feel deeply, and to pray as never before. Free to write about the many experiences that I have stored up in my heart and mind during the last nine years. Free to deepen friendships and explore new ways of loving. Free most of all to fight with the Angel of God and ask for a new blessing. The past three months seemed like a steeplechase full of complex hurdles. I have often thought, "How will I ever make it to September?" But now I am here. I have made it, and I rejoice.

The final paragraph of his final entry, Friday, August 30, 1996, reads,

A little later I was back in my own room again. It was full of flowers...There were many balloons and large welcome-home cards with the names and drawings of many community members. What a night! What a warm welcome! Indeed, the sabbatical year is over, and it is good to be back. [Nouwen (1998) 3, 222]

HISTORY

No commandment is more intricately interwoven in God's covenant with Israel than the edict to keep the Sabbath. It makes its first appearance at the beginning. When God finished creating the cosmos, he rested on the first-ever Saturday. In resting, "God declares as fully possible just how very good creation is. Resting, God takes pleasure in what has been made; God has no regrets, no need to go on to create a still better world or creature more wonderful than the man and woman. In the day of rest, God's free love toward humanity takes form as time shared with them." [Bass 78] In other words, God has no need to go on creating, and by ceasing his work, he established the six-days-of-work, one-day-of-rest pattern that has guided Judaism ever since.

Sabbath comes from the Hebrew word *shabbat*, which means 'to cease.' Israel's neighbors knew nothing of a day of rest per week—the Babylonian calendar had certain days where work stopped because the date was deemed evil—so Israel stood out for having this day dedicated to worship, prayer, and leisure.

Having escaped the seven-day-per-week drudgery of slavery in Egypt, God quickly reminded Israel of the importance of keeping Sabbath. When the manna fell from heaven during the exodus, Moses advised the Israelites to gather only enough for one day, one omer; they quickly found that when they gathered more, it rotted. However, on the sixth day, Moses told the people to gather two omers worth of manna, since there would be no manna on the seventh day. Sure enough, some of the more anxious Israelites went out on the seventh morning to collect manna, and there was none. Upon their return to camp, Moses was scolded by the Lord, "'How long will you refuse to keep my commandments and instructions? See! The Lord has given you the sabbath, therefore on the sixth day he gives you food for two days; each of you stay where you are; do not leave your place on the seventh day.' So the people rested on the seventh day." [Exodus 16:28-30 NRSV]

Not long after that, God delivered the Ten Commandments to Moses, the commandment to keep the Sabbath being the longest. In Exodus, it reads,

Remember the Sabbath day by keeping it holy. Six days you shall labor and do all your work, but the seventh day is a Sabbath to the Lord your God. On it you shall not do any work, neither you, nor your son or daughter, nor your manservant or maidservant, nor your animals, nor the alien within your gates.

For in six days the Lord made the heavens and the earth, the sea, and all that is in them, but he rested on the seventh day. Therefore the Lord blessed the Sabbath day and made it holy. [Exodus 20:8-11]

In this reading, the command to "remember" the Sabbath is linked to God's creation of the world.

The version in Deuteronomy is somewhat different, for it focuses on the Israelites' release from their nonstop work as slaves:

Observe the Sabbath day by keeping it holy, as the Lord your God has commanded you. Six days you shall labor and do all your work, but the seventh day is a Sabbath to the Lord your God. On it you shall not do any work, neither you, nor your son or daughter, nor your manservant or maidservant, nor your ox, your donkey or any of your animals, nor the alien within your gates, so that your manservant and maidservant may rest, as you do. Remember that you were slaves in Egypt and that the Lord your God brought you out of there with a mighty hand and an outstretched arm. Therefore the Lord your God has commanded you to observe the Sabbath day. [Deuteronomy 5:12-15]

Elsewhere in the Pentateuch, details of the Sabbath observance are recorded: sacrifices may be offered, psalms may be sung, and the royal guards may be changed, but there was to be no food gathering, plowing or reaping, starting fires, or chopping wood.

And the prophets invoked the fourth commandment more than any other. Ezekiel equates this commandment to all God's other commandments; Jeremiah proclaims that the fate of Israel depends on its ability to keep the Sabbath; Isaiah exclaims that it's the primary decree of God, linked to the salvation of the nation:

If you keep your feet from breaking the Sabbath
and from doing as you please on my holy day,
if you call the Sabbath a delight
and the Lord's holy day honorable,
and if you honor it by not going your own way
and not doing as you please or speaking idle words,
then you will find your joy in the LORD,
and I will cause you to ride on the heights of the land
and to feast on the inheritance of your father Jacob."
The mouth of the LORD has spoken. [Isaiah 58:13-14]

With all of this Old Testament material, it's no wonder that

Sabbath keeping was a litmus test by the time Jesus came along. To the Pharisees' way of thinking, Jesus was lax in his observance of the Sabbath, healing people on the holy day and allowing his disciples to pluck ears of corn. One of the Pharisees' primary complaints was that Jesus claimed to be "Lord of the Sabbath" and proclaimed, "The sabbath was made for humankind, and not humankind for the sabbath." [Mark 2:27 NRSV]

Early Christians, especially those of Jewish descent, struggled with Sabbath keeping. Many still observed the Sabbath on Saturday, and celebrated Jesus' resurrection on Sunday. In 321, the Emperor Constantine decreed Sunday instead of Saturday to be a day of no work, but of worship of the Lord, thereby effectively changing the Sabbath to the first day of the week.

In the time since, both Jews and Christians have been guilty of "Sabbatarianism"—that is, excessive strictness in the observance of the Sabbath. Even in Jesus' day, Jewish leaders were doing battle over what it meant to rest from work on the Sabbath. The Jewish Sabbath is observed from sunset Friday through sunset Saturday. Rabbis decided, after reflecting upon Exodus 35:5, that 2,000 cubits (just over half a mile) was a "Sabbath day's journey"—walking farther than this would be considered "work" (at the modern excavation of Gezer, stones have been found marking this boundary around the city). [Acthtemeier 955]

However, as the people lived with this law, they began to push the rabbis on the definition—what could they get away with legally? You can imagine the conversation:

"Okay, so I can walk 2,000 cubits from my home on the Sabbath."

"Correct."

"Well, if I were to eat a majority of my meals at another place, wouldn't that be considered my home for the day?"

"Hmm, I suppose."

"So, if I were to walk 2,000 cubits on Friday afternoon and leave two meals there on the road, that would be my temporary home for the Sabbath."

"I guess"

"Then, on Saturday morning, I could walk those 2,000 cubits to my temporary home, and then another 2,000 cubits beyond to my friends' home. I will have walked 4,000 cubits without having done any work, technically speaking."

"Alright, alright!"

In fact, that's pretty much what happened. If a person planned it out right, he could get just about anywhere he wanted on the Sabbath and still stay within the law by laying out meals along the way on Friday afternoon. To this day, Orthodox Jews deal with similar issues. Turning on a light switch is considered work in Orthodox Judaism because lighting a fire or lamp was forbidden in the ancient Sabbath laws. One may, however, open the refrigerator on the grounds that any electrical current produced in the process is incidental and without express intention.

However, Sabbatarianism isn't solely the purview of Jews. Three times in the history of the Reformed church, for instance, theologian-politicians have legislated strict Sabbath-keeping laws and heavy punishments for those who break the laws: first in the English and Scottish Reformation of the 17th century, then in the Evangelical Revival of the 18th century, and again during the Prohibition era of the 20th century.

Poking around on the Internet, one finds dozens of court cases, editorials and letters to the editor, and elections in which so-called "Blue Laws" are at issue even today. These are the laws that prohibit commerce, especially involving alcohol and tobacco, on Sunday. The debate rages that these are legalisms based on a strict Puritan desire to enforce moral behavior on everyone, that it's a church-state separation issue. In any case, one gets the feeling that the battle to force our culture to observe the Sabbath was lost 50 years ago.

THEOLOGY

Notably, Jesus did not say, "Forget about the Sabbath, it's an old, dead tradition, void of meaning and relevance." No, he said (and his actions indicated) that while the spirit of the law holds, there is a new, higher allegiance—discipleship—that takes precedence.

Now, with the coming of Christ, the Sabbath has taken on new meaning. As well as pointing backward to creation, it points forward to the rest and peace we will have in Christ when he comes again. Thus, early in the church the Sabbath was shifted to Sunday—the day of Jesus' resurrection. And instead of being bound with legalistic obligations, it became known as the "feast day of the Lord." Sunday became a day for Christians to gather for worship, prayer, and a big *agape* meal, including the Lord's Supper.

Theologian Jurgen Moltmann writes, "If we sum up the commandment and the reason for it, we get the following picture: God creates and shapes a rich and colourful world in order to celebrate the feast of creation with all his creatures on the Sabbath. Therefore the Sabbath is the consummation of creation; without it creation is incomplete and remains insignificant." [Moltmann 282] And as we celebrate it weekly, we have hope in God's final consummation—the return of Christ!

This, then, is the way of observing the Sabbath that's truest to Scripture: obedience to God's command that we observe the Sabbath day and keep it holy—that we maintain the Sabbath as a day of joyful worship and Communion, a day of rest, and a day of reliance upon God. "To act as if the world cannot get along without our work for one day in seven is a startling display of pride that denies the sufficiency of our generous maker." [Bass 86]

A related concept sheds light on the theological importance of Sabbath. The Law of Moses prescribed that for one out of every seven years, fields were to be given a "Sabbatical Year" to lie fallow. [Exodus 23; Deuteronomy 15] Not only did this preserve the nutrients in the soil and remind the people that the land was not theirs but God's, but it was also commanded that any crops that did grow during the Sabbatical Year were to be left for the poor and the wild animals. [Exodus 23:10-11] So the Sabbatical Year commandment was not only good agricultural policy, it also shaped the moral identity of Israel.

PRACTICE

Jewish scholars have debated for centuries what should and should not be done on the Sabbath:

What should not be done is "work." Defining exactly what that means is a long and continuing argument, but one classic answer is that work is whatever requires changing the natural, material world. All week long, human beings wrestle with the natural world, tilling and hammering and carrying and burning. On the Sabbath, however, Jews let it be. They celebrate it as it is and live in it in peace and gratitude. Humans are created too, after all, and in gratefully receiving the gift of the world, they learn to remember that it is not, finally, human effort that grows the grain and forges the steel. By extension, all activities associated with work or commerce are also prohibited. You are not even supposed to think about them. [Bass 80]

Instead, the Sabbath is to be a day of activities like worship, prayer, family time, lovemaking, naps, and walks.

The thought of trying to practice this in our own lives could hardly seem more countercultural. As our world "speeds up" and people work more, weekends have become the primary time for shopping, mowing the lawn, paying bills, and even for holding church committee meetings.

And for those of us who work on Sundays, keeping a Sabbath looks even more impossible—especially considering the constant needs of our students (and our constant need to be needed!). Yet, there's an alternative. I remember hearing a tape by Mike Yaconelli years ago in which he told new youth workers to take a full day off. "I take my wife to a motel," Mike said. "We bring a bottle of wine, a couple of novels, and we take the phone off the hook. No one knows where we are. What if a kid shows up at the church in crisis? There are other pastors on the staff who are trained to help people—I figure they can handle it."

Pastor extraordinaire, Eugene Peterson, says he protected himself (and his spouse) from congregational exploitation by keeping a Sabbath:

Monday was a Sabbath. My wife and I would spend the day in the woods quite regularly. I told my congregation what I was doing. About every three years I'd write a pastoral letter explaining "why your pastor keeps a Sabbath." In time they started to see me as a person who had needs, which I was taking care of. And they started to recognize and respect the fact that I was not simply someone who was available to them all the time, but someone who, on Mondays, was out in the woods watching birds." [Wood 21]

Keeping a Sabbath isn't a practice that can be achieved slowly, bit by bit, over time. There must be, at some point, a radical break. Decisions must be made by the youth worker (and her family), and they must be articulated clearly to the congregation. As at Gezer, the boundary stones must be set, never to be moved or walked beyond. I can tell you from personal experience that one abruptly ended phone call at home on a Saturday (one of my days *off)* will quickly become known around the congregation, and the phone calls on your Sabbath will dramatically dwindle.

A regular sabbatical is another item to demand when you start working at a church. The majority of this book was written during a three-month sabbatical, and I can't overstate the wonderful impact that the time away from my church had on my soul. Whether you're a professional youth worker or a diligent volunteer, ceasing your work and your ministry is biblical. Push your elder board, your senior pastor, your boss to give you a sabbatical. Scour the employee handbook for the sabbatical policy, and if there isn't one, write one up and pro-

pose it at the next church meeting.

8 p.m.—I'm on the plane to London. This morning at church was a bittersweet experience. So many people had read my letter to the congregation explaining my sabbatical, and they wished me well, said I'd be in their prayers, etc. But it was very sad to say goodbye. Three months without seeing these people will be difficult, I think. For good and ill, the people of Colonial Church, in part, define who I am. Like any pastor, my ability to help them gives me worth, for it fulfills my calling.

It was surprising how many times I was tempted to say, "Oh, that's alright, you can call me." I told a couple of people, "You can contact me, but not as a pastor; only as a friend." They both responded: "When have I ever contacted you as a pastor?" I doubt this makes me unique as a pastor.

I have definitely felt anxiety as this trip and this sabbatical have approached: How much will I miss my family while I travel? Will Julie and I really be able to get along for two months in close quarters? Am I really ready/worthy to write a book on spirituality? How much of who I am is being a pastor—that is, will I find out things about myself that I don't want to know while I am away from being a pastor?

Most of the Easter worship this morning was a blur. What will it be like to worship without being in leadership for three months???

THOUGHTS FOR YOUTH MINISTRY

If you really want to get in trouble with parents, challenge your students to keep Sunday as a Sabbath: no soccer games or hockey tournaments, no working at a part-time job, no shopping, no homework. Propose that Sunday be devoted exclusively to things like worship, family brunch, watching the football game, taking a nap, family dinner, and youth group or small group. Then sit back and watch the fireworks. Watch parents, especially those who know the biblical mandate for Sabbath keeping, try to defend their families' habits and their children's schedules. And watch students struggle with the way of the world versus the way of Jesus.

Of course, your students could get all their homework done on Friday and Saturday and they could decline to work the Sunday shift, but it will probably be so far from anything they've ever considered that it will take a while for them to regain trust that you are a lucid human being. From there, set up accountability structures and reporting techniques to assist them in their practice. And encourage them as they constantly fail in their attempts, because they will fail.

Two reminders, however, are imperative. First, don't let it become legalistic. And second, you'd better be practicing Sabbath keeping in your own life before you challenge your students with it.

A FINAL WORD

Theologian Jürgen Moltmann writes,

The Sabbath opens creation for its true future. On the Sabbath the redemption of the world is celebrated in anticipation. The Sabbath is itself the presence of eternity in time, and a foretaste of the world to come. [Moltmann 276]

Chapter 18
Service

Without love, the outward work is of no value; but whatever is done out of love, be it ever so little, is wholly fruitful. For God regards the greatness of love that prompts a man, rather than the greatness of achievement.

Thomas à Kempis

Aimee is a college student in Kansas City, and she wrote this:

As an insecure and lonely 15 year old, I had no real reason to go on the spring break mission trip other than to meet people and feel better about myself. I had few friends and was struggling to find my "place"—that group where I would magically connect, belong, and be loved. Maybe this trip to Juarez, Mexico would be just the thing I needed to make friends with the kids in my youth group.

Not quite. I felt isolated almost the whole trip; everyone else, it seemed, had their best friends and did not want another. Building houses for impoverished people in Juarez did not even bring the satisfaction I had anticipated. Something was still missing.

I had chalked the trip up as a loss by the time we had our last group meeting on the night before we were to return. Wrong again. The director of the trip talked to us about John 13 and Jesus' lesson to his disciples about service. Then our leaders did the strangest thing: they lived out Jesus' call to wash one another's feet. Emerging from the kitchen armed with tubs of soapy water and a towel, they proceeded to wash the stinky, sweaty feet of all 35 high school kids. I can only describe what happened when my turn came as a mystical experience. It all suddenly became so clear; the pieces of the gospel message and the experiences of the past few days began to fall into place. I realized in that moment what service is really about: Jesus is real, and he loves ME.

Six years later, I found myself leading a group of high school students on a similar trip with the same mission organization. This time I had the chance to wash the feet of other people and see the light of recognition go on in their hearts. Jesus' message of service and sacrifice continues to be the most influential, amazing, life-changing thing I have ever encountered.

HISTORY

Friends and colleagues who knew I was writing a book on spiritual practices had one overwhelming word of advice: "Please be sure to include a chapter on service." The fear, it seems, is that a book on spiritual disciplines, especially contemplative ones, will encourage navel-gazing—that is, that contemplatives might look inward to the exclusion of serving others.

The history of the church proves otherwise. From the earliest days, the leaders of the church took seriously Jesus' call to serve others. There is, for instance, the famous description of the church in Acts 2:

All who believed were together and had all things in common; *they would sell their possessions and goods and distribute the proceeds to all, as any had need.* Day by day, as they spent much time together in the temple, they broke bread at home and ate their food with glad and generous hearts, praising God and having the goodwill of all the people. And day by day the Lord added to their number those who were being saved. [Acts 2:44-47 NRSV, emphasis added]

Similarly, Acts 4 tells of believers selling their possessions and laying the proceeds at the disciples' feet, and Acts 6 recounts the choosing of seven deacons to look after the needs of widows and others in the community.

Every period of history since has had saints who were not only theologically astute and renowned contemplative pray-ers, but who were also servants:

→ The Desert Fathers and Mothers, the archetypical contemplatives, never thought their years in the wilderness were self-serving. Instead, they spent their time there praying for the needs of the world—and they also knew that whatever they learned about God in the desert was meant to be shared with the church.

→ In his Rule, Benedict of Nursia (480-547) wrote that even cloistered monks are to take in strangers who come to the abbey: "When, therefore, a guest is announced, let him be met by the Superior and the brethren with every mark of charity. And let them first pray together, and then let them associate with one another in peace.… In the greeting let all humility be shown to the guests, whether coming or going; with the head bowed down or the whole body prostrate on the ground, let Christ be adored in them as he is also received." [ch. 53]

→ In the Middle Ages it was contemplative monks and nuns

who cared for and took in persons dying of the Plague, even at the risk of their own lives.

→ Francis of Assisi (1182-1226) is famous for shedding his expensive clothes in the town square and covering himself with a burlap sack. He and his fellows took a vow of poverty to show their own humility before the Lord and to be able to work on behalf of the poor with no thought for their own well-being.

→ Dietrich Bonhoeffer (1906-1945) was ultimately executed for helping Jews to escape the Nazi concentration camps.

→ Mother Theresa (1910-1997) became world renowned for her work among the poor and lepers in Calcutta.

In every era, the church has done its best work when it has looked outward. All of the best theology is empty without an ethic of service, an ethic that Jesus so explicitly instituted. Thousands of missions, hospitals, and universities have been founded to serve in Jesus' name. Millions of Christians have taken the call to servanthood seriously and stepped out of normalcy and cultural comfort. And innumerable billions of acts of kindness take place every year as followers of Christ serve with no intention of seeking recognition or repayment.

THEOLOGY

The Bible passages that exhort believers to service in the Lord's name are too numerous to mention, so we will concentrate on one passage:

Then the mother of Zebedee's sons came to Jesus with her sons and, kneeling down, asked a favor of him. "What is it you want?" he asked. She said, "Grant that one of these two sons of mine may sit at your right and the other at your left in your kingdom."

"You don't know what you are asking," Jesus said to them. "Can you drink the cup I am going to drink?"

"We can," they answered. Jesus said to them, "You will indeed drink from my cup, but to sit at my right or left is not for me to grant. These places belong to those for whom they have been prepared by my Father."

When the ten heard about this, they were indignant with the two brothers. Jesus called them together and said, "You know that the rulers of the Gentiles lord it over them, and their high officials exercise authority over them. Not so with you. Instead, whoever wants to become great among you must be your servant, and whoever wants to be first must be your slave—just as the Son of Man did not come to be served, but to serve, and to give his life as a ransom for many." [Matthew 20:20-28]

John Chrysostom (c.347-407) wrote of this passage, "Do you see how everywhere Jesus encourages them by turning things upside down?" [Simonetti 118] And, indeed, Jesus subverts the common knowledge of ours and every age by teaching that the real way to lead is to serve.

Actually, throughout his earthly ministry, Jesus proves by example time and time again that servanthood is the key to the Kingdom of God about which he's teaching. He teaches that God cares for us so much that he numbers the hairs on our heads; then Jesus exemplifies that divine love by healing a blind man, a leper, a woman with an issue of blood. In most kingdoms, the rulers act like the Gentiles to whom Jesus refers, but in God's kingdom, the first will be last.

Richard Foster writes that this is leadership not with a scepter, but with a towel. When Jesus washed his disciples' feet at the Last Supper, he was performing the ultimate act of service to them. Then, after rising, he said to them, "I have set you an example that you should do as I have done for you." [John 13:15] There's no wiggle room in that statement, or in the declaration, "…whoever wants to become great among you must be your servant, and whoever wants to be first must be your slave." [Matthew 20:26-27] Jesus makes no bones about it: Christians serve. Period.

It's day three out in the field in Quiquijana, Peru. Today we spent most of the day building guinea pig pens—one out of wood and five out of adobe bricks—in people's homes. That is, if you can call them homes. One of the places we worked is an adobe structure that might be 10 feet by 10 feet inside. A 90-year-old man lives there, alone. He sleeps on a pile of blankets next to a little fire in which he burns wood and trash. A little walled area adjacent to his home was probably a foot deep with animal dung from wall to wall.

The team that worked on the pen in this home painted a poignant portrait tonight at devotions: almost every one of them, upon seeing the feces they were going to have to wade through as they carried bricks back and forth either thought or said, "You've got to be kidding me." That is, until one of their number said, "This is being a servant!" Suddenly their perspectives changed and the rest of the day was actually a joy...regardless of the footing.

PRACTICE

Servanthood is so foundational to the Christian life that it's hard to know where to begin talking about the practice of it. Everything from doing the dishes at home to washing someone's feet to donating one of your kidneys to your brother is within the spectrum of service in Jesus' name. For most of us, on most days, Jesus is calling us to tasks somewhere between doing the dishes and donating a kidney—the trick is determining what Jesus is calling me to today.

That's where service intersects with all of the aforementioned practices. For centuries, the Christians who were known for their service to the world were also those Christians who took their spiritual development seriously. When we take time and make space for God to move in our lives, we then have the resources necessary for true servanthood. Ultimately, how you serve Jesus and God's creation is a reflection of your personal spiritual health.

So practice the disciplines and watch yourself become a servant.

THOUGHTS FOR YOUTH MINISTRY

Within the Kingdom-building work of youth ministry, the opportunities for service are almost overwhelming. For example, Youth Specialties lists more than 120 links on its Web site to mission organizations offering trips for students and groups. Most youth workers see great benefit in making service and mission a centerpiece of their ministries.

Before becoming a youth pastor, I worked for a student mission organization. For three years I organized, planned, and ran mission trips for youth groups, most of them on the Pine Ridge Indian Reservation in South Dakota. I came to the conclusion during that time, and I still believe today, that nothing changes students' lives like a mission trip. There's just something about taking students someplace else, away from their normal environment, and challenging them to serve, that has an impact.

Like any of us, students need to be shocked sometimes, to see how other people live in order to be reminded about the priorities of the Kingdom of God. Resources abound to help you set up service projects or mission trips for your youth group—take advantage of them!

A FINAL WORD

From Richard Foster's *Celebration of Discipline*:

More than any other single way, the grace of humility is worked into our lives through the Discipline of service. [Foster 130]

Developing a Rule of Life

All cannot use the same kind of spiritual exercises, but one suits this person, and another that. Different devotions are suited also to the seasons, some being best for the festivals, and others for ordinary days. We find some helpful in temptations, others in peace and quietness. Some things we like to consider when we are sad, and others when we are full of joy in the Lord.

Thomas à Kempis

Ultimately, the application of these or any ancient spiritual practice is up to the individual Christian, because, while some practices hold deep meaning for one person, a different set of practices will appeal to another. And, as Thomas à Kempis notes in the opening quote, different seasons in our lives call for different disciplines.

However, it's vitally important that each believer develops a "Rule of Life"—that is, "a pattern of spiritual disciplines that provides structure and direction for growth in holiness." [Thompson 138]

As has been noted often, we live in an era that's lacking in *discipline*—in fact, *discipline* is a dirty word, at least in reference to spirituality. Athletes are encouraged to be disciplined in their diet and workouts, and musicians in their rehearsals, but spiritual discipline is often seen as oppressive.

On the contrary, spiritual discipline is liberation, for it's within the time set aside to be disciplined that we are changed and shaped by God. The ultimate goal in life for a Christian is that we become *conformed to the image of Christ*. Spiritual discipline is the time-tested arena for that change.

Many areas in our life are desperately in need of discipline. And youth workers are notorious for a lack of discipline in life: unpredictable work patterns often lead to bad sleep, diet, and exercise habits. Self-discipline in any of these areas can (and probably should) be spiritual. Any time you've gone for a run when it was the last thing you wanted to do or passed up a dessert, it has probably tested your spirit! (In fact, I received a good word before I wrote my first book: "Writing is a spiritual discipline," my pastor told me. I have found that to be very true. As I write this it's 5 a.m.! It took everything I've got to crawl out of bed and fire up the computer this morning. Writing is indeed a discipline for me, and it's an important part of my Rule of Life.)

It may be writing or journaling, it may be exercise or diet; as you examine your life, you may see many areas that need discipline. The best idea is to start with two or three areas of discipline, and add to them gradually as you experience some success.

Another way to achieve some success is to orient your Rule around the Christian calendar. Try one discipline during Lent, another during Advent. Use the Lectionary, a three-year daily cycle of Scripture reading, to guide your practice of *lectio divina* or the Daily Office. The church year has certain cycles and patterns that are immensely helpful for the spiritual life.

Following some experience with the ancient practices outlined in this book, you may decide to incorporate some of them into your personal Rule of Life. An example of a rule could look something like this:

→ Pray through two centuries of the Jesus Prayer in the morning and evening every day.

→ Keep the Sabbath from sunset Friday to sunset Saturday every week.

→ Walk a labyrinth once a month.

→ Take a two-day silent retreat once a year.

→ Fast and walk the Stations of the Cross every Friday during Lent.

→ Take a 28-day Ignatian retreat every decade.

You will naturally be more attracted to some practices than others. It is best to start with the ones that are to your liking, but after some time it's good to examine why others are less enticing and venture into them. Over the span of your life, your Rule will change, as well.

In addition to a personal Rule of Life, corporate Rules can be established. We've already looked at the most famous, the *Rule of St. Benedict*. Your youth group could develop its own Rule, determining the practices that are expected of members of the ministry. This might include, for example, daily sacred reading, weekly corporate worship, quarterly service projects, and an annual silent retreat. The team going on the summer mission trip could institute a Rule for the three months of preparation and the week of the trip. It's best for the group to determine the Rule, rather than have it imposed by a single leader.

Ultimately, as a youth pastor, my Rule of Life is far more important than the model I have adopted for the ministry or how well I recruit volunteers or whether I'm a dynamic communicator. "The spiritual life is not something we add onto an already busy life…. [It] is to impregnate and infiltrate and control what we already do with an attitude of service to God." [Nouwen and Foster 112] My Rule is the starting point for ministry—without a Rule, my ministry isn't coming from a deep reservoir of the Holy Spirit but from my own limited human strength.

We have lots of options in our ministries, but developing a disciplined spiritual life isn't one of them. That is, it isn't optional. It's mandatory. And, it's life giving!

Slow down. Listen to God. Be silent. Meditate. Make the Stations. Stare at an icon.

And, there, do you feel it? The divine light of the Risen Christ flickering within you, slowly building to a roaring fire…

THE FINAL WORD

Thomas à Kempis has guided us throughout our exploration of ancient spiritual practices, and we turn to him once more for a prayer that induces humility in all of us who teach and write:

O God, living Truth, unite me to yourself in everlasting love! Often I am wearied by all I read and hear. In you alone is all that I desire and long for. Therefore let all teachers keep silence, and let all creation be still before you; do you, O Lord, speak alone.

BOOK RESOURCES

Sacred Reading

Boa, Kenneth, *Historic Creeds: A Journal,* Colorado Springs: NavPress, 2000 (117 pp.) and *Sacred Reading: A Journal,* Colorado Springs: NavPress, 2000 (115 pp.). After a good introduction about *lectio,* each book has 90 readings and related questions following the four-part process of reading. This could definitely be used in a youth ministry setting.

Casey, Michael, *Sacred Reading: The Ancient Art of Lectio Divina,* Ligouri, Missouri: Ligouri, 1995 (151 pp.). A Cistercian monk in Australia, Casey sketches the theology and practice of *lectio,* along with a final chapter on reading some traditional texts.

Meisel, Anthony C. and M. L. del Mastro (translators), *The Rule of St. Benedict,* New York: Doubleday, 1975 (117 pp.). As well as the Rule, the translators provide a nice introduction with a history of the monastic movement.

Pennington, M. Basil, O.C.S.O., *Lectio Divina: Renewing the Ancient Practice of Praying the Scriptures,* New York: Crossroad, 1998 (148 pp.). Pennington is on the forefront of the contemplative movement and he provides an excellent understanding of *lectio.*

Silence and Solitude

Merton, Thomas, *The Silent Life,* New York: Farrar, Strauss, and Giroux, 1957 (178 pp.). Ten years after taking monastic vows, Merton reflected on the silence of the life he had chosen, and the union with Christ that had resulted.

Nouwen, Henri J.M., *The Way of the Heart,* New York: Ballantine, 1981 (81 pp.). This little devotional book has become a modern classic, using the Desert Fathers as guides for a contemporary spirituality.

The Jesus Prayer

Bacovin, Helen (translator), *The Way of a Pilgrim and The Pilgrim Continues His Way,* New York: Doubleday, 1978 (194 pp.). A modern spiritual classic, this work is by an anonymous 18th century Russian wayfarer. After a troubled life in which he is injured beyond his capability to work and his young wife dies, the Pilgrim sells all and wanders the Russian countryside attempting to fulfill Jesus exhortation to "Pray without ceasing." He is told by a spiritual director to use the Jesus Prayer as the basis of his life. This book is very readable, plus it has an appendix with teaching on the Prayer by early church fathers.

Kadloubovsky, E. and G.E.H. Palmer (translators), *Writings from the Philokalia on Prayer of the Heart,* London: Faber and Faber, 1951 (420 pp.). A collection from the great writings of the Eastern Fathers that mirrors the selections read by the anonymous author of *The Way of a Pilgrim.*

Mathewes-Green, Frederica, *The Illumined Heart: The Ancient Christian Path of Transformation*, Brewster, Massachusetts: Paraclete, 2001 (112 pp.). An adult convert to Orthodoxy, Mathewes-Green imagines a fifth century Eastern Christian, Anna, and examines the routines of her life to glean lessons for us today. Short and wonderful. She has a nice list of group study questions on her Web site: www.frederica.com.

Centering Prayer

Anonymous, *The Cloud of Unknowing* (William Johnston, ed.), New York: Doubleday, 1973 (195 pp.). An anonymous 14th-century treatise on mystical prayer, *The Cloud* is the first mystical classic in English. The author took up the theme of nonintellectual prayer common with many Desert Fathers and applied it as advice from a spiritual father to his disciple.

Keating, Thomas, *Open Mind, Open Heart: The Contemplative Dimension of the Gospel,* New York: Continuum, 2002 (148 pp.). Keating is a Cistercian priest, monk, and abbot who writes a nice history of contemplative prayer in the first chapter and then goes on to teach the principles of Centering Prayer.

Pennington, M. Basil, O.C.S.O., *Centering Prayer: Renewing an Ancient Christian Prayer Form*, Garden City, New York: Doubleday, 1980 (222 pp.). Pennington, a Trappist monk, is a leading authority on Centering Prayer. A retreat leader, speaker, and writer, this is his magnum opus on the Prayer; he also coauthored the more recent *Centered Living: The Way of Centering Prayer* (which is available free online at www.lectiodivina.org). Both books trace the history of the Prayer, develop it theologically, and give sound and practical advice on its practice.

Meditation

Balthasar, Hans Urs von, *Christian Meditation*, San Francisco: Ignatius, 1989 (97 pp.). A short theological treatise on meditation by a giant of 20th-century Catholic theology.

DeMello, Anthony, *Wellsprings: A Book of Spiritual Exercises*, New York: Doubleday, 1985 (240 pp.). Combining the traditions of the East and the West, DeMello, a Jesuit priest, offers poetry based on Scripture that leads the believer on a journey.

Main, John, *Moment of Christ: The Path of Meditation*, Continuum, 1998 (128 pp.). Benedictine monk John Main combined Christian teaching with Hindu meditation to form a mantra-type meditation. This and other books are compilations of his teachings—he formed communities for meditation in Ealing, England and Montreal, Canada.

The Ignatian Examen

Ignatius of Loyola, *The Spiritual Exercises of Saint Ignatius* (translated by Pierre Wolff), Triumph: Liguori, Missouri, 1997 (236 pp.). Wolff, a former Jesuit and frequent retreat leader, translates the Exercises into an easily readable American version, and he has helpful notes on each section based on his experience at leading retreats.

Linn, Dennis, Shelia Fabricant Linn, and Matthew Linn, *Sleeping with Bread: Holding What Gives You Life*, Mahwah, New York: Paulist, 1995 (73 pp.). The authors lead Ignatian retreats in hospitals and at retreat centers; they have seen many people deeply affected by ending the day by meditating on that day's consolations and desolations. Francisco Miranda's illustrations give this work the look and feel of a children's book and, indeed, the authors intend to show how simple this practice can be to develop.

Icons

Forest, Jim, *Praying with Icons*, Orbis: Maryknoll, New York, 1997 (171 pp.). A friend of Dorothy Day, Henri Nouwen, and Thomas Merton, Jim Forest has traveled in heady theological company. But he left the Catholicism that he shared with those three when he and his wife discovered the potency of prayer with icons. The book shares his journey and what he's learned.

Hallick, Mary Paloumpis, *The Story of Icons*, Brookline: Holy Cross Orthodox Press, 2001 (80 pp.). A former middle school teacher, Hallick wrote this book for students. It's easy to read, has some good pictures, and gives examples of important feast days.

Jenkins, Simon, *Windows into Heaven: The Icons and Spirituality of Russia*, Oxford: Lion, 1998 (64 pp.). This is like a miniature coffee table book. It gives a nice introduction to the theology and spirituality of icons; then each major feast is introduced with a reflection, an ancient prayer, and a full-page, full-color glossy picture of an icon.

Nouwen, Henri J.M., *Behold the Beauty of the Lord: Praying with Icons*, Notre Dame, Indiana: Ave Maria, 1987 (80 pp.). Collected here are Nouwen's reflections on four different icons, along with fold-out pictures of each icon.

Spiritual Direction

Aelred of Rievaulx, *The Way of Friendship*, New York: New City Press, 2001 (168 pp.). This spiritual classic lays the groundwork for spiritual friends to listen for the Spirit in one another's lives.

Barry, William A. and William J. Connolly, *The Practice of Spiritual Direction*, San Francisco: HarperCollins, 1981 (209 pp.). Both Barry and Connolly are Jesuit priests who were involved the rebirth of SD during the 1970s. They trained SDs at the Center for Religious Development in Cambridge, Massachusetts for years, and this book presents their combined wisdom.

Guenther, Margaret, *Holy Listening: The Art of Spiritual Direction*, Boston: Cowley, 1992 (146 pp.). Guenther wrote this modern classic on spiritual direction after years of being an SD, professor, hospital chaplain, and Episcopal priest herself. The SD as spiritual midwife is her guiding metaphor.

Peterson, Eugene, *The Contemplative Pastor: Returning to the Art of Spiritual Direction*, Grand Rapids: Eerdmans, 1993 (179 pp.). One of the premier pastors of our time and the translator of *The Message*, Peterson encourages all pastors to make sacred companionship a hallmark of ministry.

The Daily Office

Baillie, John, *A Diary of Private Prayer*, New York: Scribner's, 1949 (130 pp.). These are the morning and evening prayers (one page each) of Baillie, a Scottish chaplain who died in 1960. They cover a month of prayer; this collection has quickly become a devotional classic.

Benson, Robert, *Venite: A Book of Daily Prayer*, New York: Tarcher/Putnam, 2000 (270 pp.). An evangelical convert to the practice of the Office, Benson arranges his book with four Offices per day, including Collects, Psalms, and Gospel readings.

Glenstal Community, *The Glenstal Book of Prayer: A Benedictine Prayer Book*, Collegeville, Minnesota: Liturgical Press, 2001 (150 pp.). This is a wonderful little prayer book that comes from the Benedictine community at Glenstal Abbey in Limerick, Ireland. As well as morning and evening prayers for each day, many of the most famous traditional prayers are recorded herein.

Tickle, Phyllis, *The Divine Hours: Prayers for Springtime: A Manual for Prayer*, New York: Doubleday, 2001 (671 pp.); *The Divine Hours: Prayers for Summertime: A Manual for Prayer*, New York: Doubleday, 2000 (512 pp.); *The Divine Hours: Prayers for Autumn and Wintertime: A Manual for Prayer*, New York: Doubleday, 2000 (651 pp.). These books are a great gift to the church. In the most readable and accessible fashion imaginable, Tickle has organized the traditional prayers for morning, noon, and evening, replete with Scripture texts and prayers ancient and modern. Monthly Compline prayers are also included. These books have become my guide for daily prayer.

Webber, Robert (translator and adaptor), *The Prymer: The Prayer Book of the Medieval Era Adapted for Contemporary Use*, Brewster, Massachusetts: Paraclete, 2000 (172 pp.). Webber, the dean of evangelicals who have embraced the pre-Reformation rhythms of church life, has translated the most widely used prayer book of the 15th century for 21st century use. The book is divided into the eight Daily Offices, but it is also adaptable for a week or a month retreat.

The Labyrinth

Artress, Lauren, *Walking a Sacred Path: Rediscovering the Labyrinth as a Spiritual Tool*, New York: Riverhead, 1995 (199 pp.). After an experience at Chartres, Artress went back to her job and started utilizing a labyrinth at Grace Cathedral in San Francisco. The popularity of her project surged and labyrinths have been popping up around North America ever since. This book details her journey.

Hartwell Geffrion, Jill Kimberly, *Praying the Labyrinth: A Journal for Spiritual Exploration*, Cleveland: Pilgrim, 1999 (112 pp.) and *Living the Labyrinth: 101 Paths to a Deeper Connection with the Sacred*, Cleveland: Pilgrim, 200 (87 pp.). Both of these are journals that guide you in walking the labyrinth with Scripture and then ask you to journal your thoughts about the journey.

Stations of the Cross

Nouwen, Henri, *Walk with Jesus: Stations of the Cross,* Maryknoll, New York: Orbis, 1990 (98 pp.). After Nouwen was hit by a car while hitchhiking, he was given drawings of the Stations by Sr. Helen David to reflect on while recuperating in the hospital. The drawings represent the Stations through the suffering and oppression of the world's poor, and Nouwen's devotions reflect his many travels to places of poverty.

Pilgrimage

Brancatelli, Robert J. *Pilgrimage as Rite of Passage: A guidebook for Youth Ministry*, New York: Paulist, 1998 (66 pp.). This is a practical guidebook and a healthy combination of ideas and theory. It's aimed specifically at Roman Catholic youth workers, but could be easily applied elsewhere.

Sabbath

Bass, Dorothy, "Keeping Sabbath" in *Practicing Our Faith: A Way of Life for a Searching People* (Dorothy C. Bass, ed.), San Francisco: Jossey Bass, 1997 (232 pp.). Bass' chapter is the best in an all-around excellent book. She uses the history and theology behind the Sabbath to construct a reasonable practice in today's world.

Dawn, Marva, *Keeping the Sabbath Wholly: Ceasing, Resting, Embracing, Healing,* Grand Rapids, Michigan: Eerdmans, 1989 (234 pp.). One of our best practical theologians weighs in on the practice of Sabbath keeping—as always, Dawn is witty and challenging.

Muller, Wayne, *Sabbath: Finding Rest, Renewal, and Delight in Our Busy Lives*, New York: Bantam, 1999 (241 pp.). Muller spells out beautiful and practical ideas that, though rooted in the Judeo-Christian tradition, are applicable to all spiritual people.

Service

Youth Specialties, *Ideas: Camps, Retreats, Missions & Service Ideas*, Grand Rapids, Michigan: Zondervan, 1997 (89 pp.). A practical workbook of ideas for planning and running your own mission and service events.

WEB RESOURCES

General Sites on Spirituality and Spiritual Practices

www.ccel.org The Christian Classics Ethereal Library, an unparalleled collection of the great writings of the Christian tradition—if it's in the public domain, they've got it.

www.newadvent.org A major Catholic Web site hosting the entire Catholic Encyclopedia online.

www.sfts.edu Using a grant from the Lilly Endowment, the Youth Ministry and Spirituality Project has as its mission: "To foster Christian communities that are attentive to God's presence, discerning the Spirit, and that accompany young people on the Way of Jesus." In many ways, the people involved in this project are setting the course for the future of youth ministry.

Sacred Reading

www.lectiodivina.org This is a fantastic site with loads of resources and links and some really informative articles. In fact, there is even the class assignment for some freshmen at a Catholic high school in Milwaukee who write about *lectio* for class.

The Jesus Prayer

www.easternchristian.com/ropes Various prayer ropes for reciting the Jesus Prayer are sold here.

Centering Prayer

See www.centeringprayer.org The Web site of Contemplative Outreach, Ltd., an organization that provides retreats and seminars on centering.

See www.lectiodivina.org (above).

Meditation

www.innerexplorations.com This site is "Where Christian mysticism, theology, and metaphysics meet Eastern religions, Jungian psychology and a new sense of the earth." It's got good information defending John Main's style of meditation.

www.christianmeditation.com This is a commercial site that sells tapes and CDs for guided meditation.

www.wccm.org The World Community for Christian Meditation continues the work of John Main from its offices in London. This site hosts bulletin boards, event listings, and books and tapes.

The Ignatian Examen

www.sacredspace.ie The Web site of the Jesuit Communication Centre in Dublin, Ireland. Millions have prayed through a daily Ignatian prayer since this site debuted in 1999. *Sacredspace* is the gateway for Ignatian prayer in over a dozen languages and the Kansas City-based youth ministry organization, YouthFront, has launched www.sacredgateway.org using the same content with Flash media technology and more youth-savvy graphics. They promise that it will be downloadable on Palm OS devices soon.

Icons

www.christusrex.org Most of the great Christian artwork of the Western world can be accessed from this fairly unorganized site; e.g., the entirety of the Vatican's collection is here.

www.liturgica.com A Web site specializing in the art and music of Orthodoxy.

Spiritual Direction

www.sdiworld.org The Web site of Spiritual Directors International where you can look for an accredited SD in your area.

www.youthspecialties.com/special/spiritualDirection The area of YS's site devoted to spiritual direction for youth workers.

The Daily Office

www.phyllistickle.com The Web site of the author of *The Divine Hours*. Information on the books, advice on fixed-hour prayer, and links.

www.praythenews.com A site that teaches and uses contemplative prayer practices to interact with and pray for the news and needs of the world.

www.taize.fr The Web site for the Taizé community in southern France. Founded by Brother Roger, Taizé is a phenomenon in Europe, attracting thousands of youth and young adults every year. It caters to individuals and groups under 30 years of age. Every day the community gathers three times for singing (they compose all of their own music), prayer, silences, and a Scripture reading. The life of the community revolves around these thrice daily prayer services. The Taizé brothers also lead small groups in the late morning.

www.universalis.com This site is a wonder—it has daily and hourly prayer, the lectionary readings for the day, and links.

The Labyrinth

www.grace.org Grace Cathedral (Episcopalian) in San Francisco began the labyrinth revival in the mid-1990s, and, led by Lauren Artress, it is still very active today. One of the church's main projects is to collect information on every labyrinth in the world and place it into an Internet "labyrinth locator."

www.jillkhg.com Jill Geffrion is my personal labyrinth guru, and I often walk the labyrinth in her front yard that you'll see on this site. Her site is full of useful information, links, and resources for purchase.

www.labyrinth.co.uk Virtually walk the labyrinth designed by Jonny Baker and the Youth for Christ-London staff—it's featured at Youth Specialties conventions and is currently on a multiyear tour of the cathedrals of the U.K.

www.labyrinthsociety.org This site connects most of the people involved in the labyrinth revival and contains many resources.

Stations of the Cross

www.cptryon.org/xpipassio/stations Pray the Stations online.

www.robertwilson.com/studio/masterStations.htm Playwright/director/artist Robert Wilson's artistic reflections on the stations, most recently installed at Oberammergau, site of the world-famous Passion Play.

Pilgrimage

www.christian-travelers-guides.com Zondervan publishes travel books for many foreign lands with notes on all the important sacred sites in the country. A great resource.

Fasting

www.30hourfamine.org Join hundreds of thousands of Christians around the world in February, fasting for 30 hours and raising money for hunger relief.

Service

www.youthspecialties.com/links YS has links to more than 120 organizations that provide mission experiences for youth groups.

BIBLIOGRAPHY

Achtemeier, Paul J., *HarperCollins Bible Dictionary*, San Francisco: HarperCollins, 1996.

Adams, Steve, "Ancient-Modern Ministry," *Youthwork*, January, 2002, pp. 20-27.

Aelred of Rievaulx, *The Way of Friendship* (M. Basil Pennington, ed.), New York: New City Press, 2001.

Artress, Lauren, *Walking a Sacred Path: Rediscovering the Labyrinth as a Spiritual Tool*, New York: Riverhead, 1995.

Bacovin Helen (translator), *The Way of a Pilgrim and The Pilgrim Continues His Way*, New York: Doubleday, 1978.

Bailey, Jeff, "The Un-Busy Pastor: Redefining a Life Well-Lived: An Interview with Eugene Peterson," *Cutting Edge*, vol. 6, no. 1, 2002, pp. 1-4, 16-17.

Baillie, John, *A Diary of Private Prayer*, New York: Scribner's, 1949.

Balthasar, Hans Urs von, *Christian Meditation*, San Francisco: Ignatius, 1989.

Bass, Dorothy C., *Practicing Our Faith: A Way of Life for a Searching People*, San Francisco: Jossey Bass, 1997.

Bass, Dorothy C. and Don C. Richter (editors), *Way to Live: Christian Practices for Teens*, Nashville: Upper Room, 2002.

Brancatelli, Robert J. *Pilgrimage as Rite of Passage: A Guidebook for Youth Ministry*, New York: Paulist, 1998.

Cannato, Judy, "The Labyrinth: Praying Psalm 139," *Weavings*, Volume XVIII, Number 3, May/June, 2002, pp. 37-44.

Casey, Michael, *Sacred Reading: The Ancient Art of Lectio Divina*, Ligouri, Missouri: Ligouri, 1995.

Collins, Julie A., "Practical Prayer: Teenage Males Meet Ignatius Loyola," *America*, Volume 185, Number 8, September 24, 2001, pp. 7-12.

Cross, F.L. and E.A. Livingstone (editors), *The Oxford Dictionary of the Christian Church*, Oxford: Oxford University Press, 1997.

Forest, Jim, *Praying with Icons*, Orbis: Maryknoll, NY, 1997.

Foster, Richard, *Celebration of Discipline: The Path to Spiritual Growth*, San Francisco: HarperCollins, 1978.

Geffrion, Jill Kimberly Hartwell, *Praying the Labyrinth: A Journal for Spiritual Exploration*, Cleveland: Pilgrim, 1999.

Guenther, Margaret, *Holy Listening: The Art of Spiritual Direction*, Boston: Cowley, 1992.

Hallick, Mary Paloumpis, *The Story of Icons*, Brookline: Holy Cross Orthodox Press, 2001.

Hersch, Patricia, *A Tribe Apart: A Journey into the Heart of American Adolescence*, New York: Ballantine, 1998.

Jenkins, Simon, *Windows into Heaven: The Icons and Spirituality of Russia*, Oxford: Lion, 1998.

Johnston, William (editor), *The Cloud of Unknowing*, New York: Doubleday, 1973.

Kadloubovsky, E. and G.E.H. Palmer (translators), *Writings from the Philokalia on Prayer of the Heart*, London: Faber and Faber, 1951.

Kempis, Thomas à, *The Imitation of Christ*, New York: Penguin, 1952.

Kresta, Al, *Why Do Catholics Genuflect? And Answers to Other Puzzling Questions About the Catholic Church*, New York: Chatham House, 2002.

Mack, Father John, *Ascending the Heights: A Layman's Guide to The Ladder of Divine Ascent*, Ben Lomond, California: Conciliar, 1999.

Mathewes-Green, Frederica, *The Illumined Heart: The Ancient Christian Path of Transformation*, Brewster, Massachusetts: Paraclete, 2001.

McGrath, Alister E., *Christian Spirituality: An Introduction*, Malden, Massachusetts: Blackwell, 1999.

Meisel, Anthony C. and M. L. del Mastro (translators), *The Rule of St. Benedict* New York: Doubleday, 1975.

Melczer, William (translator and editor), *The Pilgrim's Guide to Santiago de Compostela*, New York: Ithaca, 1993.

Merton, Thomas, *The Monastic Journey*, Garden City, New York: Image, 1977.

————, *The Seven Storey Mountain: An Autobiography of Faith*, New York: Harcourt Brace, 1948.

Moltmann, Jürgen, *God in Creation: A New Theology of Creation and the Spirit of God*, San Francisco: Harper, 1985.

Monk of the Eastern Church, *The Year of Grace of Our Lord, Crestwood*, New York: St. Vladimir's, 1997.

Mursell, Gordon (editor), *The Story of Christian Spirituality: Two Thousand Years from East to West*, Minneapolis: Fortress, 2001.

Newman, Cardinal John Henry, *Meditations and Devotions,* London: Longman's and Green, 1893.

Norris, Kathleen, *Amazing Grace: A Vocabulary of Faith*, New York: Riverhead, 1998.

————— , *The Cloister Walk,* New York: Riverhead, 1996.

Nouwen, Henri J.M., *Behold the Beauty of the Lord: Praying with Icons*, Notre Dame, Indiana: Ave Maria, 1987.

————— , "Moving from Solitude to Community to Ministry," *Leadership Journal*, Volume XVI, Number 2, Spring 1995.

————— , *Sabbatical Journey: The Diary of His Final Year*, New York: Crossroad, 1998.

————— , *Walk with Jesus: Stations of the Cross*, Maryknoll, New York: Orbis, 1990.

————— , *The Way of the Heart*, New York: Ballantine, 1981.

Nouwen, Henri, and Richard Foster, "Deepening Our Conversation with God," *Leadership Journal*, Volume XVIII, Number 1, Winter 1997.

Pascal, Blaise, *Pensées*, London: Penguin, 1966.

Pennington, M. Basil, O.C.S.O., *Centering Prayer: Renewing an Ancient Christian Prayer Form,* Garden City, New York: Doubleday, 1980.

————— , *Lectio Divina: Renewing the Ancient Practice of Praying the Scriptures*, New York: Crossroad, 1998.

Russell, Norman and Benedicta Ward, *The Lives of the Desert Fathers*, Kalamazoo: Cistercian, 1980.

Simonetti, Manlio (editor), *Ancient Christian Commentary of Scripture: New Testament 1b: Matthew 14-28*, Downers Grove, Illinois: InterVarsity, 2002.

Thompson, Marjorie J., *Soul Feast: An Invitation to the Christian Spiritual Life*, Louisville: Westminster John Knox, 1995.

Tickle, Phyllis, *The Divine Hours: Prayers for Springtime: A Manual for Prayer*, New York: Doubleday, 2001.

Ward, Benedicta, *The Sayings of the Desert Fathers: The Alphabetical Collection*, Kalamazoo: Cistercian, 1975.

Wolff, Pierre (translator), *The Spiritual Exercises of Saint Ignatius*, Triumph: Liguori, Missouri, 1997.

Wood, David, "'The Best Life:' Eugene Peterson on Pastoral Ministry," *The Christian Century*, Volume 119, Number 6, March 13-20, 2002.

SOME DEVOTIONAL CLASSICS IN THE CHRISTIAN TRADITION

Aelred of Rievaulx (12th century): *The Way of Friendship* – a reflection on Christ-centered friendships

Anonymous (14th century): *The Cloud of Unknowing* – a mystical treatise on contemplation; the basis of Centering Prayer

Anonymous (19th century): *The Way of a Pilgrim* and *The Pilgrim Continues His Way* – a Russian wayfarer discovers the Jesus Prayer during his journeys

Aquinas, Thomas (13th century): *The Aquinas Prayer Book: The Prayers and Hymns of St. Thomas Aquinas* – one of the greatest theologians of all times at prayer

Athanasius (4th century): *The Life of St. Anthony* – the biography of a Desert Father

Augustine of Hippo (4th-5th centuries): *The Confessions* – the greatest spiritual memoir of all time

Baillie, John (20th century): *A Diary of Private Prayer* – thirty-one daily devotions by a Scottish pastor

Benedict of Nursia (6th century): *The Rule of St. Benedict* – the foundation of the Benedictine way of life and spirituality

Bernard of Clairvaux (12th century): *On the Love of God* – a treatise on how to love God and how God loves us

Bonhoeffer, Dietrich (20th century): *The Cost of Discipleship* – a classic on self-sacrifice in Jesus' name

Bonhoeffer, Dietrich (20th century): *Life Together* – his reflection on how Christians need to live in the world and with one another

Brother Lawrence (17th century): *The Practice of the Presence of God* – the diary of a Carmelite monk who experienced God's presence daily

Brother Ugolino (13th century): *The Little Flowers of St. Francis* – a biography of the great medieval saint

Bunyan, John (17th century): *The Pilgrim's Progress* – a metaphor of our journey through the temptations of life

Catherine of Genoa (15th century): *The Spiritual Dialogue* – a reflection on the soul's purgation and movement toward God

Catherine of Siena (14th century): *The Dialogue* – the dictation of an ecstatic experience with sections on divine providence, discretion, prayer, obedience

Chambers, Oswald (19th-20th centuries): *My Utmost for His Highest* – a collection of 365 of his devotional writings

de Sales, Francis (16th-17th centuries): *Introduction to the Devout Life* – a meditation on following Christ in the secular world

Desert Fathers and Mothers (4th-19th centuries): *Lives of the Desert Fathers* – a collection of stories of the lives of the desert hermits

Desert Fathers and Mothers (4th-19th centuries): *Sayings of the*

Desert Fathers – a collection of their sayings on fasting, silence, prayer, and many other categories

Desert Fathers and Mothers (4th-19th centuries): *The Philokalia* – a collection of their sayings and writings regarding the Jesus Prayer

Eckhardt, Meister (13th/14th centuries): *Collected Works* – a mystical treatise on the intersection between Greek philosophy and Christian theology with an emphasis on God's indwelling of humanity

Fénelon, François (17th century): *Meditations on the Heart of God* – advice on developing intimacy with God by seeking after his heart

Fox, George (17th century): *The Journal of George Fox* – the spiritual memoir of a Quaker leader who was persecuted, yet retained his faith and belief that all humans have access to God

Hammerskjöld, Dag (20th century): *Markings* – journal entries from a Secretary-General of the United Nations who worked for world peace out of his Christian convictions

Hildegard of Bingen (12th century): *Scivias* – description and explanation of 26 mystical visions she received from God, uniting, for the first time, mysticism and doctrine

Ignatius of Loyola (16th century): *The Spiritual Exercises* – the 28-day retreat during which a believer examines his own life and moves toward unity with Christ

John Climacus (7th century): *The Ladder of Divine Ascent* – the handbook for eastern monastics, it portrays the Christian life as a ladder, each rung a virtue to be mastered

John of the Cross (16th century): *The Dark Night of the Soul* – an ecstatic poem that traces the soul through its purgation of sin toward union with God in divine love

Julian of Norwich (14th century): *Showings* – her 16 revelations of God's love, including some beautiful imagery of God as divine Mother

Kelly, Thomas (20th century): *A Testament of Devotion* – five essays by a Quaker teacher about finding the peace of God's presence in the midst of a noisy life

Kempis, Thomas à (15th century): *The Imitation of Christ* – possibly the greatest spiritual classic ever written, a mediation on following Christ with humility

Lewis, C.S. (20th century): *Mere Christianity* – an apologetic classic on what it means to believe in and follow Christ

Merton, Thomas (20th century): *The Seven Storey Mountain* – the spiritual biography of the 20th century's most famous monk

Merton, Thomas (20th century): *New Seeds of Contemplation* – Merton's classic treatise on the contemplative life

Nouwen, Henri J. M. (20th century): *In the Name of Jesus* – Nouwen's reflections on the trials and joys of Christian ministry

Nouwen, Henri J. M. (20th century): *The Way of the Heart* – short devotions on the three bases of the contemplative life: solitude, silence, and prayer

Pascal, Blaise (17th century): *Pensées* – a collection of his notes and essays on science, the weakness of our humanity, and the wager of faith

Schaeffer, Francis A. (20th century): *True Spirituality* – living a life in Christ in the midst of the modern world, focusing on the redemptive power of his resurrection

Teresa of Ávila (16th century): *The Interior Castle* – her account of building one's soul toward perfection and thus making it a dwelling place for God

Thérèsa of Lisieux (19th century): *The Story of a Soul* – the autobiography of a mystic who battled illness, died young, and is considered by some to be the great modern saint

Underhill, Evelyn (20th century): *The Spiritual Life* – an outline of the spiritual life and cooperation with God by arguably the greatest mystic of the 20th century

Weil, Simone (20th century): *Waiting for God* – excerpts of journals, letters, and essays by a convert to Christianity from Judaism who attained almost daily mystical union with Christ

Woolman, John (18th century): *The Journal of John Woolman* – the spiritual autobiography of a early Quaker who emphasizes revolution through peace and harmony